Saving Our Teen Drivers: Using Aviation Safety Skills on the Roadways

How to Avoid the 13 Most Common Ways Teenage Drivers Kill Themselves

John H. Loughry

Seminee Publishing, Ltd.

Contents

Disclaimer

This book was written with the sole purpose of providing information related to driving safety. It is sold with the understanding that the author and publisher are not rendering driver education, driver training, or parenting guidance.

This manual is designed to provide summary information and make readers aware of the ample research available on driver safety and crash analysis. You are urged to read all available material and use this information for your specific needs.

Every effort has been made to ensure the completeness and accuracy of this manual. Be advised that it may contain both typographical and content mistakes and as such, information contained within should be used as a general guide.

This manual was written to entertain and educate. Drivers will encounter dangerous situations requiring fast and accurate defensive reactions. There is no possible way this manual can cover all possible scenarios that a driver will encounter. Therefore, readers are urged to use the information contained within this manual as input from which to make their own driving decisions.

If you do not want to be bound by this disclaimer, you may return this book to the publisher for a full refund.

Introduction

Fatal driving accidents remain the leading cause of teenager deaths in the United States. Add to this alarming statistic the fact that 80 percent of fatal driving accidents are attributed to poor and inappropriate decisions and it is easy to understand why newly-licensed and inexperienced drivers are so vulnerable. Any method or tool that parents can use to improve the odds of their child's safety needs to be taken advantage of.

Sure, your new driver will attend driver education, read textbooks on the mechanics of driving, learn the regulations, and most likely spend time with you as a supervisory adult driver. This is a good start. But from the first driving lesson on forward, emphasis needs to be placed on the importance of having the proper driving attitude, making better decisions while under pressure, and increasing the odds of avoiding accidents.

As a Commercial airplane pilot, I have a passion for safety and have been trained to make fast and accurate decisions while under pressure. My twenty-five years of aviation experience allow me to share a different perspective on driving safety, especially for young and inexperienced drivers. This book was written to supplement the standard driver education and driver training. It blends information from government crash reports and independent driving safety studies with the practices of relevant safety training and decision-making coming direct from the cockpit.

This combination of information is made relevant to driving situations and is repackaged for you, the parent. These skills have helped me avoid numerous dangerous surprises that always seem to find a way of happening at the most critical and inopportune moments. In addition to improving my overall safety performance as a pilot, these skills have helped me to avoid two very close mid-air collisions as well as manage an on-board electrical fire, engine failure, and multiple instrumentation failures.

While in college, I worked as an emergency medical technician on a rescue squad and witnessed firsthand the devastation that can overtake a family when one of their members is killed in a driving accident. Drunk drivers, speeding teenagers, and the occasional driver that was just plain incompetent often found someone to hit. The concept for this book started during my rescue squad days. I immediately saw a correlation between my pilot training and skills that might give a driver that extra second or extra bit of knowledge to make a better, more appropriate accident avoidance decision.

I named my concept PilotDriver because the goal was to take pilot skills and transfer them to drivers, turning them into PilotDrivers. But like many ideas it remained a vision that never materialized due to other projects with higher priority. Then in 2000, I overheard a conversation that rekindled that old PilotDriver concept.

The question of why drivers' errors are responsible for 80 percent of accidents was running around inside my head for several days after seeing a news report about some local teenagers who were killed in a car accident involving two cars. One car was carrying two teenage boys. The driver was under the influence of alcohol. His speeding car slammed into a car carrying four sober teenagers. Police reports indicated the second car appeared to be operating responsibly and the four teens were "minding their own business." Only the passenger of the drunk driver survived the crash. This was a perfect example of how irresponsible drivers continuously shatter the lives of innocent people. It reminded me of my rescue squad days and my PilotDriver concept.

The following week, I was driving home after completing a flight. I clearly remember it being an exceptionally challenging flight. The last 45 minutes were particularly rough due to deteriorating weather, turbulence, and heavy air traffic congestion. Everyone was scrambling to get on the ground before an approaching storm hit. After a turbulent approach, I broke out of the clouds just at the minimum descent altitude (about 200 feet above the runway), found the runway, and landed in extremely windy conditions. This particular flight definitely presented one of the more challenging approaches and landings I've made. It was the type of flight that keeps a pilot humble.

After completing my paperwork and securing the plane, I got in my car and started my usual 45-minute drive home. The storm had moved in and there was heavy rain, lightning, and lowered visibility. I pulled into my regular gas station for fuel and my usual post-flight soda. A conversation inside the gas station caught my attention; I overheard a mother and her teenage "driver-in-training" daughter discussing how uncomfortable and unsafe both of them felt driving in this weather.

I silently chuckled to myself, thinking, "This is nothing. Try dodging thunderstorms in an attempt to land a fast-moving plane, in limited visibility, with heavy turbulence, while simultaneously looking for a short, fog-hidden runway. This drive home in my car, on the ground, with a little rain is nothing." The mother was giving her daughter feedback during a break from their driving lesson. The mother commented that she felt her daughter had made some incorrect decisions when a driver cut them off in an intersection. The daughter responded that she had never been taught how to react in a panic situation, to which the mother replied, "Neither have I."

This mother/daughter conversation combined with the news report I heard the previous week about the drunk driver revived the old, and dusty, PilotDriver concept. My hope is that some information from this book will resonate with you and will be passed along to your young driver as part of the mentoring and parenting process. Think of this as a parent's guide to reducing the 80 percent driver decision error—from a pilot's point of view

A few housekeeping thoughts as we move forward.

1. A knowledge transfer has to take place in order to understand and appreciate the pilot techniques we will apply to improving driver safety. After this initial discussion, we will then dissect the thirteen most common ways teenage drivers kill themselves and how piloting techniques can be utilized to improve safety. With awareness of these techniques and some practice, they will become second nature and will start to happen frequently. This is a good thing.

2. Drivers of all ages and all skill levels are likely to encounter the same scenarios we will cover. Statistics confirm that what we will be covering are the more common causes of teenage driver accidents, but these same dangerous situations can happen to any driver at any time.

3. It takes time for the government to gather, validate, report, and publish most of the data I have used. By the time a report is published, the data is already at least a few years old but is in fact the most current data available. I have used several of these studies to help validate the most common vulnerabilities.

4. Flying is a very safe mode of transportation. But aviation accidents do happen and it is these accidents I will be focusing on. Pilot error is attributed to a large percentage of aviation accidents. Of the relatively small number of aviation accidents, compared to overall flights and certainly as compared to automobile accidents, the percentage involving pilot error as a contributing factor is high.

Chapter 1
The Young Driver
Accident Crisis

Statistics

Data reported by the U.S. Department of Transportation's National Highway Traffic Safety Administration on young drivers states:[1]

- Motor vehicle accidents are the leading cause of death for drivers age 15 to 20.
- Traffic accidents overall account for approximately 2 percent of all deaths. But for drivers age 15 to 20, they are responsible for over 35 percent of deaths.
- Newly licensed drivers who are 16 years of age have a crash rate three times as high as that for 18- to19-year-old drivers and are twenty times more likely to be involved in an accident than all other drivers.

A big misconception is that the "younger driver" is a teen just starting to drive on a learner permit or is a 16-year-old newly licensed person. However, a large amount of supporting data confirms that many deadly motor vehicle crashes involve young drivers in the 16- to 20-year-old age range. This stems from multiple reasons. The most common are:

1. **Inexperience.** Relatively speaking, learning how to physically control and manipulate a vehicle from one place to another does not take that long to figure out and manage. However, driving a vehicle in conditions with multiple occurring events requires a higher level of competence and experience in making split-second driving decisions. Young drivers lack experience with previous driving situations upon which to base decisions. They also

lack experience in making fast and accurate decisions while under pressure from external forces that are outside of their control. This lack of previous experience, knowledge, and decision-making capabilities leads to driving errors.

2. **Immaturity.** Some drivers of all ages exhibit signs of driving immaturity and irresponsibility. There are some adult drivers who drive more recklessly than young drivers. Overall, however, people in the teenage driver population are still maturing and wrestling with how to balance the increased demand for more responsible behavior with the desire to enjoy their freedom and expand their boundaries. They are learning how to act in a more mature and responsible manner. A by-product of this learning process is making mistakes, including errors in judgment. Immaturity in this sense boils down to irresponsibility. Speeding, driving while impaired, and engaging in reckless behavior are just a few examples of serious errors in judgment that are all too common. Ironically, whether or not to commit any of these three irresponsible acts is directly under the control of the driver.

3. **Peer pressure.** Many young drivers are susceptible to peer pressure—probably more susceptible than many parents realize. Taunting friends and idolized individuals usually have the clout to pressure a young driver into acting in a manner that they would otherwise consider dangerous and inappropriate. Peer pressure spawns risky behavior, which in turn leads to driving errors.

4. **Testing boundaries.** Many young drivers take driving seriously and approach driving with a strong sense of maturity and responsibility. They do, in fact, recognize that responsibility goes hand-in-hand with driving a vehicle. Young drivers quickly become comfortable in handling a vehicle under ideal and normal driving conditions without having to deal with external threats from a drunk driver or tailgating maniac. With a quick comfort level established, it is normal behavior for young drivers to expand their boundaries and try new experiences. Pushing limits is, after all, how one gains further experience, and from new experience comes knowledge. However, trying a new driving skill or reacting to an unfamiliar situation may lead to a mistake.

Your parenting instincts and responsibilities encourage you to take ample time to educate and discuss in depth with your young driver how to handle a car and traffic rules as well as to go to painstaking lengths to emphasize the impact that inexperience, immaturity, peer pressure, and testing boundaries can have in making poor decisions. You also emphasize that these poor decisions, in turn, lead to driver errors, which in turn can result in accidents or death.

Many young drivers take their responsibilities seriously and truly do make an attempt to do everything within their power to drive safely. For this diligent and noble effort to work, safe driving practices must be followed 100 percent of the time with no exceptions. However, the chances of keeping this behavior up full time is extremely unlikely. Assume for a moment that your teen is a safe driving teen: Does she remain relentless and 100 percent focused on her safety as well as the safety of her passengers and bystanders? Is she truly safe?

Any driver, regardless of his responsibility and maturity level, is very much at risk of injury or death due to the actions of other irresponsible drivers. Assuming we can get our children on board with responsible driving, we, as parents, still have a demanding job to educate them on all of the other things that might happen to jeopardize their well-being. It is not a fair world and it is not a safe driving environment; everyone is at risk.

How many times have you seen a news report on a young driver who was operating her vehicle safely and doing everything right yet was killed by another driver? The fact needs to be burned into permanent memory that despite your best efforts to instill safety and responsibility and despite your young driver's best attempts to execute this knowledge, every person on the road, regardless of whether they are a driver or a passenger, remains in constant danger due to the reckless and stupid acts of other drivers.

I have talked with many parents on the subject of younger driver responsibility and the conversation usually ends with a stunned look of panic and realization that no matter how safe a driver is or attempts to be, they still remain at constant risk of being hit by another driver, experiencing a tire blowout or brake failure, or any one of an infinite number of unexpected situations.

We will discuss strategies later on how to help young drivers avoid making irresponsible decisions as well as strategies for helping the responsible driver avoid a dangerous encounter with an irresponsible driver. It is essential to understand and manage variables that are within a driver's control and to recognize and react to those variables that are not in a driver's direct control. Airplane pilots do this constantly without even thinking about it since a fast moving airplane requires fast and accurate decisions. It is second nature to pilots since dealing with other aircraft, weather, air traffic control, and a mixture of other dynamic variables constantly forces a pilot to make precautionary and reactionary decisions. My goal is to educate parents and young drivers to constantly think with the same mindset that pilots use. I want to empower you with the knowledge and tools that pilots have at their disposal. I want to better educate your young driver on how to increase his or her odds of staying safe by thinking like a pilot. I want to empower parents by increasing your knowledge and in turn transforming your young driver's thinking process. By transplanting relevant pilot skills into the thinking process of your young driver, together we can transform him or her into a PilotDriver.

Groups like Mothers Against Drunk Driving (MADD) and Students Against Drunk Driving (SADD) as well as the government's participation in public awareness and crash study research have done a good job in starting to address the particular issue of alcohol-related driver accidents. A tremendous focus has been put on the prevention of driving while impaired by alcohol and/or drugs. These and other organizations have done a great job of playing a role in lowering the percentage of youth alcohol-related motor vehicle fatalities from 63.2 percent in 1982 to 36.6 percent in 2000.[2]

Although this trend is moving in the right direction, the percentage of deaths is still unacceptably high. In my mind, it is still 36.6 percent too high. But what about educating young drivers on the other causes of the remaining 63.4 percent of fatal vehicle accidents involving youth? Data relating to these causes is disparate and not quite as clear-cut as alcohol-related accident data, which has been compiled now for some time. In some cases, there is a lack of crash data or lack of accurate reporting; in many cases, several causes may have acted together to cause an accident while only one cause is officially recognized.

We are going to look at the thirteen leading causes of younger driver death and injury. We will categorize youth driving accidents and discuss strategies on how to prevent them as well as how to deal with the variables you can control while avoiding those variables you cannot control. I strongly emphasize the interrelationships of all these causes and variables because they usually happen in clusters. Statistical data usually tries to segregate accidents into a single cause when, in fact, there are often multiple factors leading to an accident.

One of the lessons I have learned as a parent is that as much as we love and try to protect our children, they make their own decisions when it comes to driving and other activities. We can tell our kids that it is dangerous to drink and drive and support that statement with ample facts and figures. We can continue adding to our safety stew by stirring in other accident stories, supporting data, and even some threat of punishment for good measure but each child will make his own decision on how to act. Things happen so fast while driving a car that there is usually insufficient time to recover from a single serious error, let alone a series of errors. The day a young driver sets out driving in the car alone is the day that marks her dependence on using good judgment. It all boils down to her ability to process data and make good judgments to yield the best and safest outcomes.

Driver Error

The opposite of good judgment is, of course, poor judgment. The underlying theme of this book is that poor judgment creates errors and errors create accidents. Making poor decisions that lead to errors is significant for drivers. In fact, 80 percent of all fatal driving accidents are attributed to driver error.[3] This is not surprising to me since licensing requirements are heavily concentrated on driving rules and basic vehicle operation. This curriculum is fine for the uneventful trip from home to school or from school to work but it lacks depth when it comes to anticipating, recognizing, and managing the numerous external factors that will interact, forcing a driver to make a fast and accurate decision while under pressure.

Pilot Error

The aviation community has known for some time that error in judgment leading to an error in flight is also responsible for a significant percentage of general aviation accidents. What is interesting is that the percentage of general aviation crashes attributed to pilot error is also reported to be 80 percent.[4]

The Federal Aviation Administration (FAA) mandates that pilots be educated in, among other topics, aeronautical decision making and the effects of alcohol on the human body. In addition, flight instructors and flight examiners grill pilots on emergency procedures. They often create several distractions to help teach pilots how to cope with making accurate decisions and flying an airplane while under pressure. Flight simulators are invaluable training tools for teaching pilots how to react to dangerous situations while allowing them to push their personal limits of training in a safe environment. Pilots are highly trained with hundreds or thousands of hours of flight time. They receive professional education and attend required refresher training on a regular basis. Yet, with all of this professional training and preparedness, pilot error is still the catalyst for a staggering 80 percent of general aviation accidents.

Flight phases and pilot error

Typical phases of a flight, in sequence, are:

1. Gather flight and weather information and then plan the flight
2. Follow preflight procedures and inspect the aircraft
3. Program in navigation information and prepare instruments and communication equipment
4. Taxi to the runway
5. Engine run-up, final instrumentation verification, and control checks
6. Take off
7. Climb to the cruising altitude
8. Cruise in flight
9. Descend
10. Establish approach to runway
11. Land the plane
12. Taxi to the ramp, park, and shut down the plane

Typically, the longest phase of flight is the enroute or cruise phase. The summation of the takeoff, climb, descent, and landing phases represent a relatively short amount of a flight's time. This is significant because a closer look at the pilot error data reveals that about 71 percent of general aviation accidents attributed to pilot error occur during these phases of flight that together add up to only about 10 percent of a flight's total duration.[5]

Crunch time and pilot error

It is no coincidence that taking off, climbing then descending, approaching, and landing are extremely demanding on a flight crew, let alone an airplane being flown by one pilot. During these periods, crews have a high task load requiring intense concentration, quick thinking,

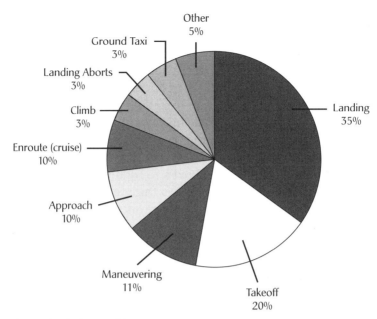

General Aviation Accidents
Sheehan, John. "Alarming Findings: Task Force Report Yields Insights into What Causes Accidents," *AOPA Pilot* (May 2003): 105–110.

and the ability to rapidly adjust to an ever-changing set of circumstances—all while flying several tons of metal through the air at both fast and critically slow airspeeds. When airplanes are taking off or landing, pilots are commanding significant speed changes which, aerodynamically speaking, require the fine touch of juggling multiple and sometimes simultaneous changes to the aircraft's configuration. Constant adjustments are made to engine settings, landing gear, flaps, trim surfaces, and so forth. To further compound a pilot's workload and make matters even more hectic, taking off and landing also typically bring an increase in traffic congestion with air traffic controllers continually making advisories and flight alterations to ensure everyone's safety. In summary, a lot of things are happening at once with an airplane moving at critically slow airspeeds, airspeeds at which there is no room for error.

In the pilot world, this high workload during critical phases of flight and emergency situations is known as crunch time. Crunch time illustrates all the decision-making variables that confront a pilot and the associated pressure to make fast and accurate decisions in rapid succession.

A Common Problem

Studies have shown that both pilots and drivers are involved in accidents because of a poor decision 80 percent of the time. Remember also that 71 percent of aviation accidents occur during just 10 percent of a flight's total duration. In an airplane, high workloads leading to task saturation contribute to stress and a deteriorating decision-making process. While automobile drivers do not have flight-oriented crunch time task saturation, they are still making mistakes and incorrect decisions at a rate equal to that of professionally trained and highly experienced pilots. My experience as both a driver and pilot is that despite the large difference between operating an aircraft and an automobile, there are some common factors and overlaps.

Pilots have numerous variables to process and decisions to make during a flight with exceptionally high peaks during the takeoff and landing phases of a flight and also during emergency situations. In addition, their workload increases during times when several situations come together such as bad weather, congested air traffic, and possibly mechanical problems.

Similarly, drivers experience a high workload when several events occur together. For example, a driver entering an intersection on a yellow light with a tailgating driver behind her on a slippery road in bad weather will likely be forced to process several variables simultaneously and select the best reaction.

Like the enroute phase of an airplane's flight, the mundane and routine enroute phase of a drive does not see the majority of driving accidents. Driving accidents usually happen during the smaller percentage of a driving trip where multiple external variables come together and interact quickly. An example of this would be driving through an intersection. Thus, similar to aviation, where a significant percentage of pilot errors occur during a relatively short but extremely critical phase of flight, many driver decision errors also take place during short but critical phases of a driving trip.

The following discussion on PilotDriver concepts will set the foundation for the conclusion of how many accidents that occur to drivers, especially young drivers, can be avoided using some basic concepts and practices that pilots have been trained in and have been using for years. I want to be clear and state that pilots are not superior to drivers when it comes to driving safety. Pilots just have different training and decision tools at their disposal when compared to the average driver with standard driver training.

I can say with confidence that there are times when every pilot struggles to stay alert and focused while juggling the many distractions and variables associated with flight. Drivers and pilots share the risk of getting caught up in a dangerous situation requiring a fast and accurate decision. As we move forward and I discuss how certain pilot strategies can assist a driver in increasing their odds of making a safer decision, keep in mind that we share this decision error risk element and are in this together.

Chapter 2
PilotDriver Concepts

I have distilled several years of pilot experience and have identified five concepts that will benefit drivers, especially young drivers who lack driving experience. The following PilotDriver concepts will lay the foundation for taking a young driver's safety, when surprised and confronted with the more common causes of younger driver accidents, to a higher level—a commercial pilot's level.

Compounding Events

One single issue or problem is usually easier to manage than two. Two are usually easier to manage than three and so on. Multiple problems often have a synergistic relationship. The attention required to process simultaneous problems is usually exponential, not linear. Trying to process and manage two situations is significantly more complicated than the sum of managing each one individually. Similarly, managing three simultaneous issues is much more complicated than managing two. It makes sense then that trying to quickly manage a situation where a driver has bad weather, congested traffic, and an aggressive driver behind him is more complicated than trying to manage bad weather one day, congested traffic on a different day, and an aggressive driver on yet another occasion.

Pilots face this same challenge—for example, managing a low fuel situation, engine trouble, and degrading weather. It creates a big situation packed with dynamic variables and complex decisions that interact. Although these are all challenging situations, managing each one individually would be an easier task than trying to manage them and all their associated complex interdependencies together.

Drivers recognizing the moment when compounding events start to materialize will prepare themselves to handle a situation sooner. First off, they make an earlier identification of when compounding events are present and second, they understand how they interact together. Being aware the instant problems start to interact and compound alerts the driver of the need to proactively take control and manage the situation.

Decision Compression

In addition to compounding events, decision compression is a second factor related to the high rate of errors made by both pilots and drivers. Decision compression occurs when the time you have available to recognize a problem, evaluate the alternatives, and make the correct decision is compressed into an extremely short time frame. Multiple interrelated variables outside of the driver's control combined with the fact that the car is moving at some rate of speed compress the available time necessary to consider all of the options.

Events associated with decision compression usually materialize quickly and take a driver by surprise. My personal piloting experience reveals that variables leading to decision compression while flying seem to happen sequentially over a short period of time, say a few minutes. They can quickly build and compound and the aware pilot can see the process start to unfold. The pilot then has a chance to prepare and get ready to manage the pending workload increase. Conversely, my experience with decision compression for drivers is that multiple events also occur in clusters, but happen in faster succession usually within a few seconds compared to a few minutes. This reduces the amount of time to begin processing the events. I believe, in general, that decision compression happens faster for drivers than for pilots and that drivers often have less warning that events are starting to compound.

Consider the following example. A driver cruising along a highway may think about changing lanes. He looks around, casually checks for other traffic and verifies the area is clear. Then he sees a car cruising up in the adjacent lane and decides to wait for this car to pass before changing lanes. Here, the driver elected to engage in a decision-making process and controlled the sequence of events in a noncompressed environment. This is a noncompressed decision because it is somewhat casual in nature; the decision-making process was initiated by the driver and electing not to change anything is an acceptable decision alternative.

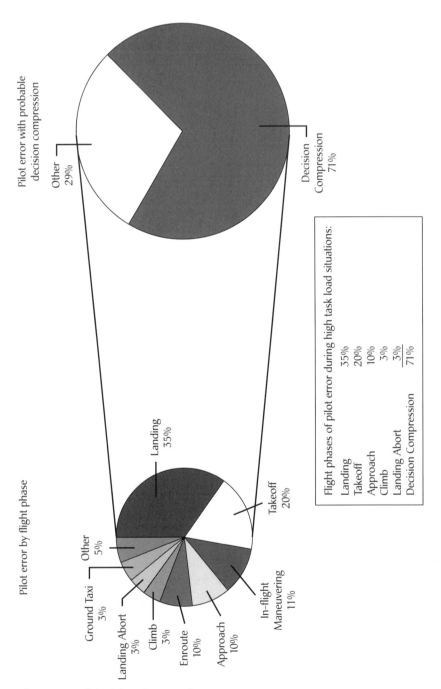

Pilot error with probable decision compression

Other
29%

Decision
Compression
71%

Flight phases of pilot error during high task load situations:

Landing	35%
Takeoff	20%
Approach	10%
Climb	3%
Landing Abort	3%
Decision Compression	71%

Pilot error by flight phase

Landing
35%

Takeoff
20%

Other
5%

Ground Taxi
3%

Landing Abort
3%

Climb
3%

Enroute
10%

Approach
10%

In-flight
Maneuvering
11%

Pilot Error and Decision Compression

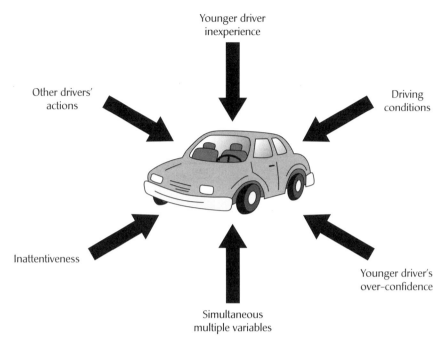

Several factors compress the decision time needed to react to a dangerous situation

Competency Silos

Over time, drivers and pilots acquire new experiences and knowledge which in turn improve their competency in performing certain tasks. A student pilot must demonstrate several times under different circumstances that she can safely land an airplane before her instructor will release her on her first solo flight.

A competency silo is not a physical structure; it is a mental attitude or belief. The word "silo" is significant because it implies that each task is well contained and separate from the others. A competency silo refers to an individual performing a certain task or completing a certain event, subconsciously declaring themselves competent and then erroneously generalizing that he or she is able to repeat that outcome again and again regardless of different circumstances. The trap for young drivers or pilots is not taking into account the many variables that will most likely change between the previous successful outcome and the next attempt. The point of competency silos is that events really cannot be mentally

Competency Silos

Can always drive safely while drinking silo. I did it once therefore I can do it again in any situation.	Can always drive safely while speeding silo. I did it once therefore I can do it again in any situation.	Can always drive safely while drowsy silo. I did it once therefore I can do it again in any situation.	Can always drive safely during distractions silo. I did it once therefore I can do it again in any situation.

Competency silos are false beliefs generalizing that experience gained from a dangerous driving act fully educates and prepares the driver in having total competency to successfully complete a similar act repeatedly

categorized and formally segregated into buckets or silos because variables in the flying world or driving world are interrelated and happen together. Events, experiences, and skills blend together with overlap in an ever-changing flow.

Sticking with our landing example, if I made a great landing yesterday, I would feel good about accomplishing the task of landing. I would then subconsciously build a silo of knowledge or belief from that successful experience and label the imaginary silo as "Landing Ability." This mental belief or "silo" now stands tall in my mind but is separate from my previously built "Takeoff Silo," "Climbing Silo," "Engine Management Silo," and hundreds of other silos relating to my previous learning experiences. The fact of the matter is that any and all of these skills could be needed at a moment's notice to manage a challenging situation. Often, multiple sources of knowledge are needed to simultaneously work together.

If I go flying again a week later and attempt to set up for another approach and landing, the circumstances are likely to be different from those encountered during the previous week's successful landing. Perhaps this time I have to contend with strong, gusty winds and sun glare on the windshield.

The competency silo trap is now set because I would erroneously think to myself, "I landed fine last week, therefore I must be competent to make the same successful landing this week." But the two landing attempts are not identical. The task of making a landing is similar but the circumstances surrounding the landing are exceedingly different. Perhaps I may have never before tried to land in severe winds or with sun glare. My generalization that I am competent to land is incorrect because today's landing circumstances are different from last week's landing circumstances.

Competency silos for drivers are identical to those for pilots. A teen may try and rationalize that since she drove and made it home safely last week after a few drinks at a party, she must therefore be competent to drink and drive. Or she must be competent at driving fast around sharp turns because she did it yesterday. Too many variables outside of a driver's or pilot's control change and this leads to false generalizations or the building of competency silos. Each driving situation must be evaluated individually and decisions need to be made for each sequential event. Individual evaluations must be done rather than just assuming that because a similar event was successfully completed, a new event can automatically be successfully completed.

A young driver needs to understand that there are two separate levels of confidence and competency. First, there is "everyday" or "normal" driving competency. Like the enroute phase of flying, this equates to performing the more simple driving tasks while not under pressure. This level of confidence builds quickly, especially in the minds of new drivers, but in actuality leads to only a small percentage of driving decision error.

A second and entirely different level of competency is required when peer pressure, alcohol, drugs, and risky behavior hinder a young driver while trying to manage compressed decisions. A higher degree of knowledge and confidence is needed to think and react under pressure. Typically, this level of competency builds more slowly than the everyday level because exposure and practice in this area often occur less frequently.

For example, a driver may have a full everyday driving experience competency silo and falsely believe he is a good driver in all driving situations. The fact of the matter is that he most likely has not yet been faced with having to make a fast or critical decision. His critical decision-making competency silo may be extremely limited or most likely, nonexistent. When faced with making a fast and critical decision, he automatically goes to his everyday competency silo to help him through. Yes, this silo is large and full of experience but its ample contents are of the wrong experiences and will be unable to assist in making a critical decision under decision compression. There is a mismatch of required skills and knowledge to available skills and knowledge. Panic usually results and the driver becomes confused.

Knowing that competency silos exist and that they create competency gaps helps create an understanding of the many driver errors that are made, especially those made under extreme pressure in dangerous situations. Just because young drivers believe that they have mastered the skills needed to drive a car under normal conditions in no way qualifies them to react under pressure to make correct emergency decisions. In fact, studies show that younger drivers usually tend to drastically overestimate their own experience level.[1]

This again is where flight simulator training is invaluable to pilots. I am talking about the multimillion dollar, multi-axis professional flight simulators, not the personal computer versions played on a home computer. Simulators were designed to allow pilots to train and make repeated attempts at performing difficult and dangerous tasks. This practice allows the pilot the opportunity to make better decisions while under decision compression. This is one way pilots proactively expand their critical decision-making competency silo while not getting injured. Making mistakes and expert debriefings about both the correct and incorrect decisions that were made in a given scenario help to better prepare pilots for handling challenging situations.

In general, young drivers rapidly build a normal competency silo, but often overstate their ability and competency. In addition, they falsely, and often unknowingly, rely on their everyday driving skills to carry them through an emergency situation under decision compression. Pilots, on the other hand, have an everyday knowledge bank and to some degree, also have a critical decision-making knowledge bank. Even with these two knowledge banks, there still exists a common 80 percent error in making decisions under pressure. This proves there are multiple factors at play; accidents do not just happen because of an individual's decision-making ability.

Task Saturation

The human brain prefers to process information and make decisions in a sequential manner. This is in contrast to computer-based simulation modeling tools that are programmed and have the necessary processing hardware to simultaneously evaluate, compare, and make a recommended outcome based on several variables in milliseconds or nanoseconds.

If you ever see a video clip of a carrier-based fighter jet like an F-18 Hornet being catapulted from the deck of an aircraft carrier, look at the pilot's right hand. By pressing a button, a crew member on the ship, not the pilot, actually launches the jet. Prior to launch, the pilot must take his or her hand off of the control stick and hold a handle near the top of the cockpit canopy. The purpose of holding this handle is for the launching crew member to visually confirm the pilot's hand is not on the control stick.

Fighter jets are extremely complex machines and when launched by catapult, things happen so fast and there are so many variables that the human brain is incapable of keeping up and accurately making the many split-second decisions required to maintain safe flight. Computers on board the fighter jet actually control the aircraft for the first few seconds after launch. Because of the numerous variables that can lead to disaster if the pilot interferes with the process, the launching crew will not initiate a carrier takeoff until they can visually confirm the pilot's hand is off of the control stick and holding onto the handle.

Pilots can face task saturation at any time but takeoffs and landings often present numerous tasks that have to happen in rapid succession. If too many tasks need to happen or the pilot falls behind in making decisions, then the task load saturates the pilot's ability to keep up and the chances of error increase exponentially.

Likewise, drivers can reach a saturation point. This occurs when the brain's ability to process data, develop an action plan, and then control the appropriate body actions cannot keep up with the demand placed on it. During normal driving, this is not usually a problem. However, when a driver is suddenly faced with an unfamiliar situation that contains several elements taking place simultaneously, decision compression will often squeeze the events together so rapidly that the brain cannot keep up, thus causing task saturation.

POP Zone Defense

A POP zone defense is a defensive strategy and risk management tool used to identify and manage three areas or zones. These three zones are known as **p**ersonal, **o**pportunistic, and **p**articipation (POP). They range in descending order based on the amount of direct control a pilot—or now you the driver—has over risks in a given situation. The use of POP zones works best when applied in a proactive thinking process prior to a drive, situation, or flight. They can, however, be used in a reactive mode for responding to a situation.

POP zone defenses can be used by drivers to take a quick assessment of any task or activity and isolate its associated risks, identify potential threats, and evoke the appropriate strategies on how to manage the situation. They assist in recognizing potentially dangerous situations early in the decision-making process. They sound more complicated than they really are and with just a little practice, you will be processing POP zones without even realizing you are doing it.

Personal Zone

The personal zone relates to the physical status of a person's body, the variables that affect a person's physical well-being, and that person's ability to control the variables that could impede the ability to perform safely. For example, a driver has direct control over deciding to consume alcohol or drugs prior to driving and is also aware that this activity will have a negative impact on the ability to perform safety.

Opportunistic Zone

The second zone is called the opportunistic zone. When a person—pilot or driver—has the ability to exert some influence in a given situation or has the ability to electively remove herself from a potentially dangerous situation, she has an opportunity to influence a safer environment. Think of the driver's opportunistic zone as involving their car and its immediate surroundings.

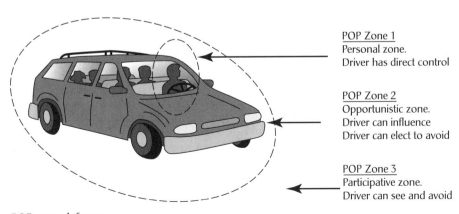

POP Zone 1
Personal zone.
Driver has direct control

POP Zone 2
Opportunistic zone.
Driver can influence
Driver can elect to avoid

POP Zone 3
Participative zone.
Driver can see and avoid

POP zone defense

For example, a person usually does not have direct control over a friend getting drunk at a party. He may be able to exert influence by reminding the friend that they rode together and want to leave together sober but he does not necessarily have direct control over the friend's actions. A good friend will intervene and hold their ground while discussing the consequences to both the drinking driver and passenger(s). If that person still elects to continue drinking, the passenger friend now has an opportunity to exert influence on a safer outcome for himself. The non-drinking friend still has the opportunity to avoid a potentially dangerous situation by electing not to ride with a drinking driver. In this case the alcohol-related situation did not negatively affect our responsible person because he initially controlled the personal POP zone by electing not to drink and drive. Second, he also controlled the opportunistic zone by subsequently electing not to ride with the impaired driver. He took the opportunity to avoid a potentially dangerous situation by being proactive in making decisions that improved his overall safety. In other words, he preemptively elected to remove himself from a situation for which he did not have direct control and improved his opportunity for safety by removing himself from the situation altogether.

The personal and opportunistic zones are proactive zones, meaning that a person should always be thinking about what threats will hurt their best and safest driving capability and then take action. It is every person's responsibility to think about these ahead of time and make safer decisions. Personal and opportunistic POP zones apply to every person whether driver, passenger, or pedestrian.

In the party situation, our model teenager took control of the personal zone by deciding not to drive while under the influence. He also managed his opportunistic zone by protecting his immediate surroundings and deciding not to be the passenger of an intoxicated driver. However, as our sober role model drives home from the party, is he really safe? What about the other intoxicated and reckless drivers sharing the same road? What if they cross paths during the trip home?

Participative Zone

The third zone, or participative zone, concerns all the other variables and situations that may coexist or participate along with a driver at some stage during a driving trip. This zone differs from the first two in that it is more reactive in nature and the driver has no direct control over the threat. The driver may have an opportunity to avoid a threat but most likely she will be forced to coexist with the threat. By being active in looking for trouble, the driver takes note of events, participating with them and trying to identify possible threats.

A pilot trying to circumnavigate bad weather or a driver just noticing a reckless driver behind him has to deal with this uninvited threat that has appeared and is now coexisting with the driver or pilot. The pilot or driver has no control over the external threat's actions, but it is in his best interest to deal with the situation in order to improve his own safety. Drivers are always living in a participative zone. This zone always exists and changes every second of every trip. Being aware of this fact should help lead to increased awareness and highlight the need to proactively look for upcoming trouble. Early detection is important to improved management of the participative zone.

Living Within the POP Zones

Pilots have, in essence, a personal checklist they go through to make sure they feel physically and mentally up for the challenge of flight. This procedure helps draw attention to their personal defense zone. They also have aircraft system checklists to ensure they have taken all possible opportunities to protect their immediate surroundings. This draws attention to their opportunistic zone. When it comes to the participative zone, it is no wonder good pilots are thinking two steps ahead, trying to anticipate unforeseen problems, identifying external threats, recognizing compounding events, and looking for other aircraft. The earlier they can identify these situations, the sooner they can decide on a corrective action to deal with events taking place within their participative zone.

No driver has full control over all of the variables that will arise and interact during a driving trip. Similarly, a pilot does not have control over every variable encountered during a flight. Drivers during or prior to each driving trip, like pilots during or prior to each flight, can use this simple POP zone defense strategy to quickly evaluate the three zones that they continuously live within and understand what upcoming activities and/or behavior will reduce their safety and within which zones they might occur.

Chapter 3
Thinking like a Pilot:
Pilot Habits for
Every Driver

As we continue to build upon these new PilotDriver concepts, there is a second level of terminology that needs to be shared before we start analyzing the most common ways teenage drivers kill themselves. There are several thinking processes that a pilot is continuously engaging in and these feed directly into PilotDriver concepts. Knowing about these processes will help as we dissect and build strategies to manage the most common teenage driver vulnerabilities.

These terms by themselves will help you to better understand how good pilots think and how even asking these questions aids in enhancing a pilot's ability to improve operational safety and decisions concerning critical or emergency situations. Therefore, starting to think like a pilot will be beneficial to drivers. Driving a car is different from flying an airplane, but the following habits will apply to drivers as well as to pilots.

Anticipation

Change is inevitable, so anticipate and prepare for it rather than trying to always react after the fact. Get into the mindset that nothing is constant. Everything changes and things are always different in some way. Try to learn to anticipate events and prepare to deal with them before they even happen.

> **Pilot.** Consider the following example. A change in wind direction might require a change in the particular runway an airport is using. It is desirable to land and take off into the direction from which the wind is blowing. As a pilot nears an

airport, she should be listening to air traffic control and paying close attention to the wind reports the controller is giving
to other pilots currently landing. Progressive reports might
hint that the wind is changing directions. After hearing the
winds are starting to change directions, the approaching pilot
might anticipate a change in the active runway. At this point,
she begins preparing to quickly react prior to actually receiving instructions from the controller to alter her course and
line up to land on a different runway. Anticipating such an
instruction allows a pilot to get the proper runway charts
ready and have the new runway's instrument landing frequencies entered and ready to use. Not anticipating such a
change ahead of time increases a pilot's workload, bringing
her closer to task saturation. It also limits her available time
to get ready for an approach-and-landing sequence.

Driver.   Drivers, too, benefit from getting into the habit of trying to anticipate upcoming events. While driving along a
highway, you notice a car gaining on you from behind. As this
speeding car passes in the adjacent lane, it rapidly approaches
a slower moving vehicle that is directly in front of it in the
same lane. The hurried car will now be forced to either slow
down to avoid rear-ending the car in front of it or cut back in
front of you. However, you, the driver who anticipates events,
will already know this speeding driver is impatient and you will
have anticipated the quick cutback in front of you. You will have
backed off just a bit to allow the reckless driver to move into
your lane. Knowing that these events are possible allows you to
be prepared with responses and corrective action.

Build Your Outs

An out is an alternate plan or an action taken to avoid or manage a situation; an action to get you out of an impending confrontation or accident. Building your outs is a natural by-product of anticipating events.
Once a potential problem is anticipated, the next logical step is to start
thinking about ways to respond to the situation.

Pilot.   Let us say the weather at a destination airport is deteriorating. The pilot might build an out by preparing to fly to an
alternate airport should the original destination's weather get

too bad to land. The alternate airport's weather may be better or it may have better instrument approach facilities for landing in poor weather.

By anticipating a situation and building an alternative plan of action, a pilot has at least one and hopefully a few alternate options in his back pocket ready to execute at a moment's notice. Thus when a situation arises, the pilot does not have to spend precious time devising an alternative. He just executes an existing alternative that was previously created. This often results in faster reaction time and faster execution time. There are rules requiring pilots to plan for and file alternate airport destinations under certain circumstances.

Driver. Just before entering an intersection, a driver scans the lanes and shoulders to either side and notes that there is a car next to her in the right lane and that the lane to her left is clear of traffic. Suddenly, it appears that a car approaching from a cross street will not be stopping as required and that it will move into the intersection on a collision path with her car. Because she anticipated this event and knew that the lane to her left was clear, she had built an out and avoids being hit by quickly moving into that left lane.

Cockpit Resource Management

Cockpit resource management is a process of organization used by experienced pilots. Aircraft cockpits are small and crowded with little room to organize the many items needed for flight. Large fold-out navigation charts (similar in size to normal folding road maps), instrument approach binders, flight computers, plotters, knee boards, and so forth are continuously needed at different phases of a flight.

Pilot. It does not take long for a cockpit to become disorganized and messy if all of these items are left lying around. More important, one good pocket of air turbulence can send items from a disorganized cockpit flying around inside, hitting people and bumping switches. Organized pilots will keep the large chart neatly folded to view only the small portion they need to see. They will keep loose items secured and will stow items not being used.

Driver.   Cockpit Resource Management applies to cars as well. Keep loose items secure and the vehicle's interior organized. Water bottles left on the car floor, for example, could be a real problem should they roll behind the brake pedal and prevent it from being depressed. A cell phone lying on the seat quickly becomes a missile when the car suddenly brakes or decelerates from an impact. Small objects become very dangerous when a car suddenly decelerates and can pack a punch of 20–30 times their weight. A passenger with a large map unfolded will often block the driver's full use of the passenger-side mirror. These little housekeeping details may seem insignificant but they are the little things that continuously show up in accident reports. After all, an accident is defined as an unexpected and undesirable event.

Err to the Conservative

You might have heard the phrase "err on the side of caution." This means if a choice has to be made, select the safer, less-risky choice. "Err to the conservative" means the same thing. While deciding upon alternative choices, pick the choice with the least severe consequence should the decision turn out to be an incorrect decision.

I made the conscious decision prior to earning my private pilot license that I would always attempt to err to the conservative. When presented with options, I always try to select the most conservative decision. This is often easier said than done but I consciously approach decisions with this philosophy and attitude. This practice has forced me to automatically recognize that if I have to debate multiple decisions, then it might be safer to stop trying to decide which one is optimal and automatically default to the safest option. This practice quickly became part of my driving decision process as well. If, for example, I have to think about whether there is enough room to pull out in front of another vehicle and into moving traffic, I do not make the move. The fact that I even had to think about and debate the option of whether or not it was safe to pull out automatically stops the decision process and I make the most conservative decision right then and there. The err-to-the-conservative decision in this case is simply not to pull out and to then wait for the next break in traffic.

Pilot.   Consider the following example. While flying, a pilot checks and verifies that there is about two hours of fuel remaining on board. Calculations show that this should be enough fuel to reach the slated destination, but it will be close. At this point, the pilot starts to consider whether the fuel calculations were accurately made, if the weather is deteriorating at the destination, if air traffic control is issuing holding-pattern assignments to other nearby aircraft, and the like. These variables might make the pilot contemplate stopping to get additional fuel before landing at the destination airport. Contemplation is significant to me and is the magical word in any decision. Any time I have to contemplate a situation and evaluate the alternatives, this is a red flag that this is an important decision with consequences and the safer decision should be made. In this case, the decision would be to stop and pick up more fuel.

The decision of whether to stop for fuel or continue along, thinking that there is enough in the tank, raises contemplation: stop for fuel or not stop for fuel. In this example, stopping for fuel is the conservative alternative and continuing on with the flight is the more aggressive alternative. The conservative and safer decision is to stop and get additional fuel. If, in fact, it turns out there was enough fuel to make the destination without stopping, then it could be said that an error was made. The error was to make an unnecessary fuel stop and lengthen the travel time. This error, however, is to the conservative alternative and it is better to be safe than sorry. Granted it is inconvenient to stop, but it is far safer than the more aggressive decision of not stopping for fuel and perhaps running out.

Driver. While approaching an intersection, your green light changes to yellow. You are forced to evaluate surroundings, evaluate options, and make a decision to either keep cruising or maybe even speed up to get through the light or else stop for the soon-to-be red light. The usual err-to-the-conservative option is to stop for the impending red light. There are exceptions, but for the most part, stopping for the red light is more conservative and less risky than trying to speed through.

Compounding Events

When more than one problem arises, they often interact, causing the problems to become more complicated and to cause distractions. Good pilots are always looking for events to start compounding together. In addition to being a pilot habit, this is also a PilotDriver concept.

> **Pilot.**   There is a saying in aviation that I have heard repeatedly over the past several years. It is a generalization: "One problem is usually manageable, multiple problems will kill you." This means once a single problem or issue arises, a pilot can usually focus on the resolution for that one particular problem and still be able to retain focus on the primary job of flying the plane. (This obviously does not apply to catastrophic problems such as an airframe failure or a mid-air collision.) When one or more problems arise simultaneously, a pilot's attention on flying the aircraft must now be reduced as some attention needs to be redirected to managing the problems. Multiple problems are often compounding and interact together. These compounding events cause distraction and often reduce the attention that can be dedicated to safely flying the aircraft.

> **Driver.**   Compounding events pose the same challenges for drivers. Attention needs to be divided between managing the problem and maintaining the safe operation of the vehicle. Drivers should be aware that two simultaneous problems are often much more challenging to manage together than if each were managed alone. Drivers usually have more congested traffic immediately surrounding them than pilots do, and this always presents a compounding problem.

> Drivers often experience compounding events in a short time period. For example, it may take only a few seconds for a driver to realize that the brakes are not working properly, the speed of the car is high, the approaching traffic light is turning red, and cross traffic does not appear to be stopping. This is a lot of data to quickly process. This is a troublesome double dose of compounding problems with decision compression.

Expect the Unexpected

Accidents, by definition, are undesirable events that occur unexpectedly. Most drivers look out for and are aware of the common things that can happen. However, it is often the uncommon or unexpected events that will surprise drivers and catch them off guard.

Pilot.　Flying an airplane is demanding, especially during take-offs and landings, because so much activity is happening. I remember flying into Canton, Ohio, one autumn day—a nice day—as I was nearing the completion of an enjoyable flight. We had been cleared to land and were close to touching down on the runway. There was a plane on the ground taxiing toward the same runway I was landing on. I heard the plane on the ground receive instructions from the control tower to taxi to the runway but hold short of the runway. "Hold short" is an official phrase meaning clearance to use the runway has not been given so the aircraft on the ground is required to stop prior to, or hold short of, the active runway. The FAA requires all pilots to repeat back to the controller all hold-short instructions. This procedure verifies for the controller that the pilot received and understood the instruction. Therefore, the pilot on the ground was required to reply and tell the Canton controller over the radio that he understood he was to taxi to the runway but stop or hold short of it. The reason he was to hold short was because I was going to land on that same runway in just a few moments.

Expecting the unexpected, I was thinking about this plane pulling out in front of me. When I did not hear the pilot on the ground repeat his hold-short instruction, I really started to expect problems. Sure enough, he taxied out onto the runway without even slowing down, forcing me to add power, retract the gear, and abort my landing. I was not happy and the controller was really unhappy, but I circled around and landed on the next approach with no harm done. Anticipating this event had me already running through the go-around procedures in my head and enabled me to quickly execute and not contemplate my next action once I saw the plane on the ground cross over the hold-short line painted on the taxiway.

There are an infinite number of things that can go wrong and you would get a headache trying to process all the possible situations that could arise to present a potential dangerous situation to you while flying or driving. The point here is to be aware that anything can happen. It also behooves one to be on the lookout for common driving dangers as well as other possible dangers from something out of the ordinary. When proactively thinking about what could go wrong next and thinking through the options, it becomes easier to identify problems when they do, in fact, occur sooner. Again, after some practice, this activity becomes second nature and is done in the background without even being aware of it.

Driver.   While stopped at a four-way intersection at night, you look around and do not see any approaching headlights. By default you might assume there are no cars coming and it is safe for you to proceed. But is it? Did you expect the unexpected? You did the right thing by looking for other cars but you expected or assumed that they would have their headlights on. If you needed to look for just headlights at night, it would be easy to determine that an intersection was clear. However, because you need to expect the unexpected, a quick secondary look for approaching cars that do not have their headlights on and are driving in the dark would be a safer move. Drivers under the influence of alcohol or drugs often forget to put their headlights on at night. Sometimes they only turn on the yellow parking lights, failing to turn on the headlights. Don't just look for moving headlights at night; expect the unexpected and look for moving cars with or without their headlights on. Street lights will illuminate a car, so look under street light areas for cars dirving without their lights on. This is especially true if you are driving around bars late at night. This is a breeding ground for cars pulling out onto the road with no lights on. Drunk drivers are careless and as you will see in the section on how to spot and identify drivers under the influence, improper use of equipment is an easy way to spot one. Unfortunately, it does become your responsibility to try to identify and avoid them.

Proactively Look for Trouble

Another pilot saying states, "If you have free time on your hands, then you've forgotten to do something." This means that there is so much involved with flying an airplane that the pilot should be constantly busy doing something. Any spare or idle time should be spent rechecking navigation equipment, refamiliarizing yourself with the approach procedures, programming radio frequencies for the next air traffic control hand off, and so forth. In essence, check, recheck, then look again for something that might be amiss. It does become habit forming and second nature after a while and this process serves to prevent errors and to correct initial errors before they become critical or compound.

> **Pilot.**   Checklists are a pilot's best friend. They provide for a systematic process of configuring the airplane for a specific task such as takeoff, cruise flight, or landing. They are especially effective when trying to troubleshoot emergency situations. Going through a prelanding check is proactively looking for trouble. It is attempting to find something that is not configured correctly. Similarly, scanning for other aircraft when approaching to land is a great way to proactively look for trouble—which leads to the ability to react in a timely manner.
>
> **Driver.**   We seem to always hear victims of vehicle accidents state, "I never saw them coming" or "I don't know where that car came from." Many drivers have a reactionary nature, meaning they drive along, jamming to tunes, thinking about weekend plans or daydreaming, and should a situation present itself, then they "snap to" and react. On the other hand, the proactive driver is looking for and anticipating trouble. They expect the unexpected. They expect the car approaching from the side street to not stop. They expect the car tailgating them to try and shoot around them in a fast-passing attempt. It will take some practice to routinely look for trouble. It will happen over time and the result will be your constant evaluation of surroundings to anticipate and identify the next threatening event.

Good pilots develop this habit quickly and it really does become second nature—it happens without even thinking about it. You will be surprised at how many dangerous driving situations you can anticipate before they even happen. You will be building your outs before other drivers even have a clue that a dangerous situation is about to unfold.

Situational Awareness

Knowing your situation and your surroundings is called situational awareness. Situational awareness is being conscious and aware of what is happening directly to you as well as immediately around you. Flight instructors push their students hard to develop situational awareness because it is a vital skill. It helps reduce mistakes and makes for a safer environment.

> **Pilot.**   Approaching to land at an airport where visibility is poor and the pilot cannot clearly see the runway, let alone the ground area, is challenging. The pilot is relying heavily on using the many flight instruments for landing guidance. In addition, as you get closer to an airport, other aircraft are also approaching. Many things happen and change very quickly. Constantly knowing your position relative to the airport is key. For example, knowing that you are 13.2 miles directly north of the destination is a start. Add to that knowing the aircraft above you is at the 2 o'clock position eastbound and another aircraft is below and behind you at the 7 o'clock position makes you aware of other traffic conflicts. Then knowing the fuel situation and what traffic flow controllers are assigning allows you to paint a mental image of your position and the surroundings. Situational awareness is having a mental image and process flow of your location, direction, and surrounding environment.
>
> **Driver.**   Drivers also will benefit from developing situational awareness, especially while driving in the vicinity of intersections, impaired drivers, and adverse weather conditions. Just like proactively looking for trouble, having a mental image of your surroundings becomes habit forming and will occur automatically. Having a mental image of what is physically around you, what variables are moving and changing, and what things are anticipated to change allows a driver to do the following three things:
>
>> 1. Compare what is happening with what they think should be happening. This creates questions and forces a driver to consider what is expected. Is the current situation different from what is expected?

2. Begin to process these differences and question if they make sense or determine that they do not make sense and therefore pose a threat.
3. Anticipate how the situation will continue to unfold while beginning to formulate a strategy for changing or avoiding the situation.

Think Two Steps Ahead

One of my favorite flying aphorisms is "always think two steps ahead." This statement means that not only should you be executing the current task but that you also need to be thinking of at least the two sequential steps that will immediately follow.

Pilot.   Things happen so quickly that the pilot must always be setting up the next needed frequency or programming the next needed navigation waypoint. Likewise, thinking two steps ahead on landing might unfold as follows: Once I land (current step), will there be enough distance to stop given current runway conditions (next sequential step), and then is there a taxiway for me to turn onto while exiting the runway (second sequential step)? Thinking about these sequential steps, it is easy to see that if the runway is icy and I am appearing to land long, I might be in trouble. Granted, I was cleared to land and I could, but I might decide not to because my thinking ahead forced me to evaluate the next event (running out of runway-stopping distance) and the next event (not having a taxiway to turn onto) before the next step actually happens.

   The Navy Blue Angels and Air Force Thunderbirds are two precision-flight demonstration teams that spend a tremendous amount of time on the ground visualizing and mentally running through their aerobatic maneuvers prior to a demonstration flight. They think several steps ahead and run through the many variables that are associated with these complex maneuvers. These exercises help them to prevent errors, quickly identify abnormal situations, and make faster decisions.

Driver.   At a party, a young driver starts to drink or take drugs. I am willing to bet every parent of such a young driver would want the child to also be thinking about the next sequential steps and consequences of getting behind the wheel. Subsequent events might include hitting another vehicle and injuring its occupants.

Thinking two steps ahead also applies when building your outs. When reacting to a threat, a driver needs to consider what will happen after she makes her first move. Swerving to avoid a vehicle could be a good thing but swerving into oncoming traffic would not be so good. Therefore, realizing you have to swerve to avoid a crash (current step) and then processing where to swerve (first sequential step) and determining if you have to stop or continue going to avoid hitting other cars (second sequential step) is good to know before you actually execute the first step of swerving.

Walk Around

While approaching your parked vehicle, take a quick walk around it and look for problems. Visually looking for abnormal indications prior to driving like leaking fluid or a tire with low air pressure presents the opportunity to deal with a problem before it compounds into a more difficult situation.

> **Pilot.**   "Walk arounds" are part of the preflight process. Unlike with automobiles, it is important to open an aircraft's fuel caps and actually look inside to verify there is not only adequate fuel but that the fuel is the correct type. Aviation fuel is color-coded. A full tank of jet fuel is deadly to a piston engine, as pistons do not take kindly to being forced to drink jet engine fuel. Checking the tires, aircraft surfaces, and control systems helps to find problems on the ground, which is better than finding problems in flight.
>
> **Driver.**   Walk arounds are simple and fast and are a good way to proactively look for problems. Aircraft walk arounds take several minutes and usually follow a detailed checklist. Automobile walk arounds are quick to perform.

See and Avoid

Look around you and see threats and dangerous situations. Then take corrective action to avoid them.

Pilot. It is always the pilot's responsibility to proactively scan the area around the aircraft to look for anything that might present a danger such as approaching aircraft during flight or perhaps an airline catering truck nearing an intersection on the airport grounds. "See and avoid" is a phrase used at every level of pilot training. Look for trouble because it is surely out there. Visually scanning the horizon and surrounding area quickly becomes a habit and is something that for most pilots is second nature.

Driver. See-and-avoid skills are also important for drivers. They go beyond just looking straight ahead as you drive; it's about looking for and trying to discover the next problem waiting for you. I believe many drivers just kind of look around at what is currently happening but are not proactively looking for upcoming trouble. When approaching an intersection, in an effort to stay safe, do not just look ahead but look for and try to uncover events that might force a defensive reaction. Perhaps there is a pedestrian, construction zone worker, road repair equipment, or some other intrusion into your driving space that offers potential for trouble. See-and-avoid skills are mandatory to successfully manage the participative zone of the POP zone defense.

Break the Trend

A series of events, whether they are good events or bad events, can string together and form a trend. Analyzing a trend may indicate a pattern of future activity. Compounding events often form positive and negative trends. People usually do not think about positive trends because they are a good thing and there is no need for reaction or corrective action—they just kind of happen in the background. Negative trends, on the other hand, can quickly compound into a serious problem or threat. Recognizing the trend and taking action to break the trend can sometimes prevent an approaching problem from evolving into an accident.

Pilot. A pilot noticing difficulty staying within the glide slope tolerance during an instrument landing approach and then being challenged to hold the proper heading is an issue. But then realizing the winds are drastically changing directions and that the aircraft's airspeed is changing—and then hearing the plane that just previously landed, telling the tower they thought they encountered low-level wind sheer—is definitely a trend and not a positive one. These compounding events most likely would indicate erratic winds and weather. At some point, the pilot might consider abandoning the approach, going around and setting up for a second attempt, or choosing an alternate landing location. Noticing that issues are starting to add up and knowing that landing is a critical stage of flight, it might be a good idea to break this negative trend of building problems and start over again.

Driver.   After a long day at work, a parent, starting to feel a bit drowsy, picks up the children at daycare. Then, the children start to quarrel loudly and begin to throw objects at each other. On top of all this, it starts to rain hard, causing reduced visibility. This is another example of a building negative trend. Noticing a negative trend, the parent should elect to break the trend and pull over for a few minutes.

Having the luxury of simply pulling over to the side of the road or into a parking lot is an option that is sometimes severely missed while flying. Compared to flying, where you just can't pull over, stop, and take a break, drivers have an easier time and ability to break trends more quickly—and this is something that should be done.

Get-there-itis

"Get-there-itis" is pilot slang and is not a good thing. It is a play on words, combining the need to get somewhere in a hurry with the medical suffix *-itis*. I list it here because it has been documented to be a factor in aviation accidents. Luckily, it is an infrequent occurrence, though surely one to be avoided. Many aviation people will agree that if a pilot does finally succumb to get-there-itis, an accident report and investigation usually follow. Get-there-itis causes a pilot to let his guard down and take chances he normally would not take because he is in a hurry to get somewhere. It can also cause a pilot to fly beyond his experience level.

Being in a rush to get to an event or home can cause a pilot or driver to perhaps overlook some safety variables or operate a vehicle beyond their capabilities in an attempt to complete a trip. They can fail to properly prepare for the journey, underestimate the effort needed to make the trip, and can overlook things that otherwise might indicate the need for caution and which under normal circumstances would delay a trip.

> **Pilot.**   Weather! Being in a hurry and wanting to avoid delays to get home after a flight or to make a destination is a big cause of get-there-itis. Pilots flying into dangerous weather or non-instrument-rated pilots flying in bad weather cause many general aviation accidents annually. In fact, flying into adverse weather without proper training or equipment is the most frequent pilot error. Many of these accidents have get-there-itis as an underlying factor because the pilot was in a hurry to complete the flight, did not want to encounter delays, and most likely flew beyond his or her experience level or beyond the aircraft's capabilities.
>
> **Driver.**   A driver that is late for a meeting, concert, date, or any of a thousand events may tend to drive a bit more quickly in an attempt to make up time. In addition, a compounding problem may be running yellow lights. Get-there-itis puts pressure on the driver to hurry up and avoid delays. This often leads to pushing the limits and assuming more risk than normal.

It is important to create a foundation of pilot knowledge from which to build on. We will continue to build upon the five PilotDriver concepts and thirteen pilot habits.

Five PilotDriver Concepts

1. Compounding events
2. Decision compression
3. Competency silos
4. Task saturation
5. POP zone defense

Thirteen Pilot Habits

1. Anticipation
2. Build your outs
3. Cockpit resource management
4. Err-to-conservative
5. Compounding events
6. Expect the unexpected
7. Proactively look for trouble
8. Situational awareness
9. Think two steps ahead
10. Walk around
11. See and avoid
12. Break the trend
13. Get-there-itis

As an emergency medical technician, I responded as a care provider to many traffic accidents and witnessed firsthand numerous accidents that I thought could have been prevented. I dissected the causes of these automobile accidents and wondered how pilot-related training might have helped to prevent each accident. It did not take long to establish that many of these accidents were caused by young drivers making reckless mistakes or young drivers getting slammed into by irresponsible adult drivers, who were often driving while under the influence of alcohol.

Could certain pilot skills have reduced some of these accidents I was responding to? This question continued to interest me over the years. After reading numerous data from organizations like the National Highway Traffic Safety Administration, National Transportation Safety Board, and the National Center for Statistics and Analysis and watching painful news reports of young driver deaths, I started to categorize accident causes into groups. The resulting summary is a list of the thirteen most common vulnerabilities that lead to young driver accidents and deaths. I want to emphasize that all drivers are susceptible to these vulnerabilities, but the young driver is especially at risk due to minimal driving experience, a natural desire to test boundaries, and inexperience in making split-second decisions while under pressure.

My goal in the next section of this book is to try to condense and combine statistical data with background research on each of the thirteen vulnerabilities. Then, once each vulnerability is discussed and validated with historical statistics, I will cross-reference the five PilotDriver concepts and thirteen pilot habits in an attempt to build awareness. In so doing I hope to help parents and young drivers identify these vulnerabilities earlier and thus avoid accidents. Hopefully, this information will you further educate your young drivers in improving their odds of staying safe.

Chapter 4
Risk Taking

Traffic accidents are the leading cause of death for young drivers 16 to 20 years of age. The percentage slightly fluctuates annually, but data supports that nearly 30 percent of all teenage deaths are caused by motor vehicle crashes.

The Fatality Analysis Reporting System, a source of data on U.S. fatal motor vehicle crashes, shows that in 2000, 53 percent of auto-related-fatalities involving people 13 to 19 years of age were drivers and 47 percent were passengers. Considering only the teenage driving years of 16 to 19, 60 percent of auto-related deaths were drivers and 40 percent were passengers.[1]

Driving while impaired is such a statistically significant cause of teenage death that it warrants its own section and focused discussion. Consuming alcohol or drugs is a double-edged sword in that it is a risky behavior in and of itself and it increases the tendency to partake in other risky activities at the same time as it slows response and reaction time. In fact, almost half of the teens in jail on assault, murder, rape, theft, and drug charges stated they were under the influence of alcohol or drugs at the time they committed their offenses.[2]

Although a teenager may not have consumed enough alcohol or taken enough drugs for her to consider herself impaired, even one social drink at a party starts to lower inhibitions and increases the chances that an individual may partake in risky driving behavior that she otherwise might not have. This increase in risky behavior, the effect of alcohol slowing reaction time and concentration, and the compounding events of other driving variables lead to high mortality rates.

Teens and young drivers are putting themselves at risk probably more often than they realize by partaking in risky behavior. For starters, teens experiment with their increasing amount of freedom. As children get older, parents allow them to start making more decisions and selecting their own actions. Many teen drivers mean well and have good intentions but occasionally overstep the very bounds they and their parents are trying to identify and manage. Parents view this flexible boundary with different and ever-changing definitions, further complicating a teen's understanding of what actions are acceptable and what actions have exceeded their responsibility boundaries. Therefore, with parents struggling with just how much freedom to give a child who is constantly trying to expand boundaries with no shortage of peer pressure, there is a great propensity toward risky behavior.

Although we as concerned, careful drivers might consider a certain driving practice risky, other drivers may not and they may therefore feel they are driving in a normal and acceptable way. Numerous studies have been conducted to see how young drivers perceive risk and what driving behavior they feel might be risky.[3] Overall, young drivers tend to view themselves as less likely to be in a crash compared to other drivers in their same age group (the "not me" syndrome).

This research indicates that young drivers tend to perceive many driving scenarios as less risky than older drivers do. In addition, young drivers are less accurate at predicting and identifying dangerous situations than older drivers partly due to their lack of driving experience. Going back to our competency silo discussion, young drivers tend not to fully comprehend that just because they successfully handled a car while speeding a little bit does not mean they can handle a car while speeding a lot.

Drivers who repeatedly engage in risky driving practices are usually trying to either show off for others or are trying to satisfy a personal desire to "live on the edge" (via thrills, excitement, and danger). Showing off by engaging in behavior that they feel people want to see is one way for a youth to satisfy a perceived need to fit in and be accepted by others. A driver in this case is attempting to satisfy the needs of others by demonstrating risky behavior that they feel other peers will think is cool.

Contrary to those who show off, some drivers do not really care about others' perceptions. They practice risky driving behavior to satisfy their own need, not the perceived needs of others. They are trying to fulfill their personal need to experience danger or reach new limits and often do so to the detriment of their passengers and other individuals nearby. Of course there are times when both factors combine and a thrill-seeking individual who likes to show off practices risky driving behavior.

Driving Motivations

The study of motivation or, in particular, driver motivation, helps to explain why some drivers engage in risky driving behavior. There are numerous types of motivation, too many to get into a long psychological discussion here. However, two worth mentioning have been studied to try to determine a correlation between motivation and risky driving behavior.

Sexual Motivation

Sexual motivation leads to an increase in risky behavior in an attempt to attract the attention of another person. A few studies suggest that sex drive and the tendency to show off may cause risky driving and affect traffic safety, particularly for males. A focus study with college students (18 to 22 years of age) documented, by self report, that one reason for drinking and driving was to show off to members of the opposite sex.[4] Young drivers who exhibit risky driving habits—driving after drinking or taking drugs, speeding, or racing—may be motivated in part by sex drive.

Arousal Motivation

Arousal motivation may help explain some of the risky driving behavior exhibited by individuals who are not showing off but rather trying to increase their own arousal as they feed their drive for personal challenge and thrill seeking. The level of risky driving needed to cause an increase in arousal is commensurate with the driver's skill level because the arousal varies with the complexity of the task.[5] Inexperienced drivers need a lower level of increased risky driving compared to a more experienced driver who will really need to raise the risky driving activity to invoke an increase in arousal.

Sensation Seeking

Numerous studies document the fact that the arousal motive can have negative consequences for traffic safety as it leads drivers to demonstrate risky driving behavior. These arousal-seeking drivers have been labeled *sensation seekers.*[6]

The goal of a sensation-seeking behavior is to increase personal stimulation by seeking varied novel, complex, and intense sensations. These experiences often result in physical, social, legal, and financial risks along with associated consequences. Thus, a sensation seeker is perhaps more interested in driving dangerously not to show off to others, but rather to increase his own physiological arousal.

Marvin Zuckerman and his associates, experts on sensation seeking studies, developed a test known as the Sensation Seeking Scale

(SSS) which has been used to help define the profile of sensation-seeking individuals and their propensity for risky driving behavior. Participants self report their behavior.

Studies show that males score higher on the total Sensation Seeking Scale than do females. In addition, the SSS score increases with age up to the late teenager years and then gradually declines as age increases. In addition, higher sensation seeking scores are related to drinking and driving for young drivers. Impaired drivers, drivers convicted of multiple driving under the influence (DUI) episodes, and those arrested for DUI following a violation or collision scored significantly higher in the SSS score than other comparison groups.

When looking at other risky driving behavior beyond driving while under the influence, studies show that those drivers who self reported exceeding the speed limit had higher SSS scores than those who did not speed. Studies also find a negative relationship between safety belt use and sensation seeking. This means that as the SSS score increased, indicating a higher desire of sensation seeking, seat belt usage decreased.

In summary, teenagers, particularly males, tend to have higher SSS scores. These scores then start to decline as age increases. In general, individuals who have a need to increase their arousal often behave in patterns of taking higher risks like drinking, speeding, and not wearing seatbelts.

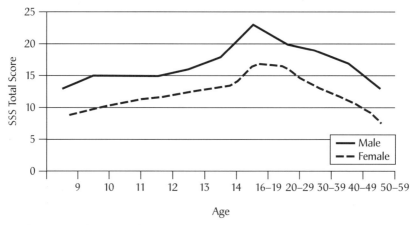

Total SSS Score by Sex and Age
National Highway Traffic Safety Administration. *Matching Traffic Safety Strategies to Youth Characteristics: A Literature Review of Cognitive Development.* Washington, D.C.: National Highway Traffic Safety Administration, 1998: 37–41.

Going back to our POP zone defense strategy, it is important to note here that the third zone, the participative zone, is the most reactionary of the three zones. Being on the lookout for dangerous drivers, those either showing off or sensation seeking, allows safe drivers and passengers to see and avoid these other drivers. Avoidance and removing yourself from the scene are the best defenses to avoid accidents.

Young Driver Bias

Young drivers tend to have some trouble with accurately assessing risk. First, they tend to only focus on seeking data that will positively support their driving habits. They fail to seek all relevant data that might, in fact, prove their driving habits unsafe. This is known as confirmation bias.[7]

Confirmation Bias

Engaging in confirmation bias is in some ways similar to performing poor statistical analysis and hypothesis testing. To reach a nonbiased conclusion, a researcher should fairly evaluate all relevant data. At the simplest level, the foundation of hypothesis testing is taking a concept that is believed to be true and trying to prove it false with sound research. The idea is to prove false what is expected to be true. The reasoning is that if methodical and accurate research fails to prove a hypothesis false, it must therefore be true. This same logic can be used by young drivers when confronting an unfamiliar scenario.

For example, say a young driver is approached by friends who want a ride home. She is driving a pickup truck and the only room available for her friends is in the back bed of the truck. If she has never encountered this request before, she will have a tendency to quickly ask herself, "Is it okay for me to give my friends a ride in the back of my truck?" As these friends anxiously peer at her, she will also have a tendency to quickly try to find a fast way to rationalize that it is safe for her friends to climb in the back bed.

Her initial reaction to this question will be to find the first scrap of data supporting that riding in the back of a pickup truck is safe. She quickly remembers that she saw other friends riding in the back of a pickup truck last week and they made it home safe; therefore it must be safe to give her friends a ride and she halts her decision process right then and there.

She quickly sets out to prove to herself that riding in the back of a pickup truck is safe and after remembering just one single instance that loosely supports it as being safe, she stopped her decision process and gave her friends a lift. She set out to prove a driving activity was safe when in fact her goal should have been to try and prove it unsafe. If she followed this course and failed to rationalize it was dangerous, she might then default to accepting it as safe. However, if she had continued thinking through the potential dangers, it would not have taken long for her to come up with some data supporting it as being a dangerous and risky behavior.

This is confirmation bias—quickly latching onto the first piece of data that tends to support a dangerous driving habit and stopping there. Parents should educate their new drivers about this tendency and impress upon them the merits of trying to prove something unsafe rather than trying to prove it safe. This comes back to the pilot habit of err-to-conservative. Eighty percent of deaths associated with driving accidents are attributed to driver error. The young woman in the example above had to make a decision. Making a decision is a red flag for careful evaluation of alternatives and also indicates that err-to-conservative decisions are most likely warranted.

Optimism Bias

Young drivers tend to think they have driving skills higher than the average driver. This is called optimism bias.[8] This bias illustrates the reason why young drivers tend to overestimate their driving aptitude. The ability of a 16- to 20-year-old driver to have skills and knowledge superior to that of an older, more experienced driver is questionable. This bias supports the competency silo illustration. Young drivers fail to realize that their experience level is stratified and the same challenge or task with different variables often yields different results.

Cumulative Risk

In addition, many young drivers fail to understand the effects of cumulative risk, especially how it relates to risky driving behavior. Drivers tend to view risk on a singular trip-by-trip basis. In reality, the experiences of each trip are cumulative. The more a driver participates in risky behavior, the more their chances increase, over time, for a violation, accident, or death. Younger drivers reason that because they completed the previous trip without an accident their driving habits must not be risky and they are safe drivers. In addition, young drivers tend to ignore the influence that external factors had on a previous trip that was completed without incident. Numerous external factors that are out of the driver's control including other drivers, road conditions, weather, fatigue, and so forth, may not have been present on a previous trip. Once again, competency silos help explain these thought processes.

Risky Behavior Tendencies

Age, experience, and individual attitude each contribute to the development of a wide range of risk perception. There are numerous situations that some people but not others consider risky. Some situations commonly considered risky are listed below. It is interesting to note that younger drivers ranked all of these situations to be less risky than did older drivers with more experience.[9]

Driving in darkness
Tailgating
Driving on curves
Driving on inclines/declines
Driving with worn tires
Urban driving
Sharing the road with a slow driver
Driving on a wet road surface
Speeding
Drinking and driving

The wearing of safety belts and being behind the wheel while driving a vehicle appear to affect the risk perception of drivers.[10] Both older and younger drivers felt that their chances of being in a crash were higher when riding as a passenger in a vehicle than when driving. This shows that people felt being behind the wheel and at the controls of a vehicle is an important factor in assessing risk. In addition, drivers who wore safety belts tended to rate the risk of accident involvement as higher than those who were not wearing safety belts. Nearly two-thirds of the passenger vehicle occupants killed in traffic crashes in 2001 were not wearing seat belts.[11]

There is also evidence that young drivers, more frequently than any other age group speed. They also speed through yellow lights, travel with a shorter distance separating vehicles, and fail to use safety belts.[12]

Seat Belt Statistics

Failure to wear a safety belt is a risky behavior. When a collision occurs and the driver or passenger inside the moving vehicle are unrestrained by a safety belt, there is a mechanical collision, a human collision, and an internal organ collision. Three separate collisions actually occur, not one. The mechanical collision is the first collision and involves the automobile striking another object. Vehicles stop suddenly, usually in less than one-tenth of a second. Bent metal, shattered glass, and items flying around inside the car are sure to result. The human collision is the second to occur and involves one or more humans continuing to move forward inside the car until they strike an object. This object most commonly is the dashboard or the seat in front of them. This second collision occurs a split second after the mechanical collision. At the moment of mechanical impact, unrestrained occupants are still traveling inside their vehicle at the vehicle's pre-collision speed.

Consider the following example. An unrestrained, 150-pound driver moving at 30 miles per hour at the time of a collision will travel forward and suffer an impact of the same force as falling from the third-story of a building. She will continue moving forward inside the vehicle, striking the object in front of her with a force of over two tons.[13]

The third collision occurs immediately after the human collision and involves the victim's internal organs colliding with other organs and/or bones. It is called the internal collision. Human organs are fragile and are often damaged when subjected to these intense internal forces.

An object's resistance to change from a state of rest or from a state of motion is called inertia. It is the force of inertia that allows an unrestrained driver to continue moving forward and hit the dashboard after a car has a collision and suddenly and rapidly decelerates. The mechanical collision followed by the human collision followed again with the organ collision often cause severe damage and death.

Isolating Risky Behavior

Being aware of and isolating risky behavior tendencies will help to reduce the variables that affect the younger driver's decision-making process and ability to safely conduct driving operations. Electing to not drive while under the influence of alcohol or drugs and not engaging in other risky behaviors should be a matter of decision and practice. Elimination of risky activities is a good thing. POP zone defense strategies work in the realm of driving because every person has the power to elect not to directly practice risky behaviors. They also have the opportunity and influence to remove themselves from riding with people who do want to practice risky behavior.

Pilots like to identify as many risk factors as they can prior to a flight and then make plans to either manage or avoid them. Flying by itself is a risky task, so why make it more complicated by not removing, identifying, or isolating risky variables associated with a particular flight? For certain types of flights, the FAA requires that the pilot conduct a thorough weather briefing to identify weather variables. In addition, they also may require a flight plan to ensure that the pilot can manage expected weather, airspace, and navigational tasks. Several scenarios require the preparation of alternate flight plans with alternate destinations because the weather often changes somewhat unpredictably. In addition, weight and balance checks, ensuring that fuel requirements are followed, and preflight instrumentation checks are all standard practices before a flight. These are all efforts to reduce variables that tend to increase the possibility of an accident.

These preflight rituals are relevant to the younger driver, although she will apply them on a much simpler scale. Prior to entering a car, the driver needs to make a fast perusal of the vehicle and any potential risk factors and then make a go or no-go decision. Factors that might be encountered on the drive such as darkness, adverse weather, construction, or drowsiness must be assessed.

It is challenging for young drivers to establish an individual driving limitations threshold. Lack of experience in driving and a lack of experience in making driving-related decisions are factors in establishing a baseline of safe operations. One way for a driver to identify driving limits is to push the comfort zone and driving habits until a limit is reached. Hopefully, the limit is not realized due to an accident or citation but instead by an experience that lets the driver know he or she has reached a limit—at least for now.

There is always risk involved in driving. The goal we are working toward is helping the young driver evaluate surroundings and driving habits and be aware of the forces that might influence a risky driving decision. We want to increase younger drivers' odds of staying safe. However, just abstaining from risky behavior is not enough to keep a driver totally safe. There are too many variables out of a driver's control and there are too many irresponsible drivers on the road who will endanger even the safest driver.

The Fatality Analysis Reporting System (2000) indicates that during the teenage years of 16 to 19, of those who die in auto-related deaths 60 percent are drivers and 40 percent are passengers. Broadening this range to include all teenagers, including those not yet old enough to be licensed to drive, the passenger fatality rate climbs from 40 percent to 47 percent.

One significant factor in the auto-related death rate is that teens often ride as passengers of teen drivers and this combination increases an already high risk rate. This combination of teenage drivers and teenage passengers tends to be a breeding ground for distractions and peer pressure which can lead to increased risky behavior. In a survey of teenagers asked to describe dangerous driving situations in which they were involved during the past 6 months, 85 percent of the reported incidents involved one or more peers as passengers in the vehicle.[14]

It is apparent that teenagers riding as passengers with teenage drivers increase the likelihood of accidents due to an increase in both risky behavior and distractions. Parents should not underestimate the exponential amount of distractions and additional task load a newly licensed driver has to contend with while chauffeuring other teenagers.

Peer pressure from the passengers perhaps adds to the driver's willingness to engage in behavior that he might not otherwise partake in. A bit less flagrant are the seemingly innocent distractions caused by passengers. For example, a driver turning her head to look back while conversing with a backseat passenger is distracted. The driver error rate for the overall driving population is 80 percent and this error rate escalates

Table 4.1 Percentage of Fatal Crashes of 16- to 17-year-old Drivers by Number of Teenage Passengers as Reported in 1999 Data from the Fatality Analysis Reporting System

Crash Characteristics	Driver Alone	Driver and 1 Teenage Passenger	Driver and 2 Teenage Passengers	Driver and 3+ Teenage Passengers
Single vehicle	32	40	44	56
Driver error	75	79	84	90
Speeding	27	37	44	48
Driver with positive blood alcohol concentration	11	12	13	20

to 90 percent when focusing on teenage drivers riding with three or more teenage passengers.[15]

Risk-Channeling Environments

Many people like to take risks. Driving in and of itself is risky when you really think about it. For many teenagers, driving also provides the freedom to push limits, expand boundaries, and partake in some level of thrill-seeking adventures.

If you feel your young driver is competitive in nature and tends to partake in risky activities with an aggressive attitude, think about encouraging their participation in an activity that allows them to channel some of their "risky behavior" energy into an organized and supervised event with proper training, supervision, and equipment.

I started to take flying lessons the week I turned 16. For me, the thrill of flying instantly superceded any thrill I thought I could derive from driving. In addition, I had a great instructor who let me constantly push my abilities. I made several mistakes while learning and pushing my personal limits and he was always there to get me out of trouble and keep me safe. I started aerobatic flight training my senior year of high school and for me, after an hour of flipping, flopping, looping, and spinning, I welcomed an uneventful and casual drive home from the airport. Flying let me channel my natural tendency to experiment with pushing my limits and take risks that perhaps I might otherwise have tried while driving. I have also scuba dived and sky dived. These are thrill-seeking events that could tame a younger driver's thirst for adventure by offering an alternative to risky behavior while driving. I have yet to find an activity that comes even close to matching the adrenalin rush from jumping out of an airplane.

Learning to fly is relatively expensive and I know many parents will question my sanity in suggesting teenagers take up parachuting as a hobby. The message is that any time someone steps outside of his normal comfort zone, he is taking risks. Channeling the desire to engage in risky behavior does not always necessitate taking up a physical activity such as flying or parachuting. If a person is somewhat shy or quiet, then a public speaking venue might offer a big risk for them. If a person has not participated in physical sports, then learning Tae Kwon Do might offer a thrilling risk. The point is that any organized and properly supervised activity that can allow a teenager to push limits and try activities considered risky might possibly limit or reduce risk-taking behind the wheel.

Review

- Teenage drivers tend to assume different combinations and levels of risk taking at different times and under different circumstances
- Multiple risk-taking activities compound exponentially, increasing the chances of an accident
- Young drivers typically misjudge the real level of risk associated with various risky driving activities
- In general, males engage in higher levels of sensation seeking than females do and also tend to be more susceptible to showing off and succumbing to peer pressure
- There is no excuse for not wearing a seat belt and those who choose not to wear one tend to partake more often in multiple risk-taking activities
- Teenage passengers of teenage drivers are also more likely to be in accidents and need to be educated on how to make smart decisions as passengers
- Relevant pilot habits and concepts that apply to risk taking are compounding events, proactively look for trouble, breaking the trend, and situational awareness

Chapter 5
Decision Making

Pilot error is responsible for 80 percent of general aircraft accidents. Similarly, driver error is responsible for 80 percent of driving accidents. I believe piloting an aircraft is more complex and demanding than driving an automobile, because there are more variables involved in controlling an aircraft when operating at high altitudes and speeds in three-dimensional space. On the other hand, I believe, in general, drivers usually have a shorter window of time in which to evaluate alternatives, make a decision, and react when confronted with a dangerous situation.

A fallacy some young drivers have is that they can maintain control over all events and thus have control over any resulting outcome. Drivers (or pilots) only have control over how they perform their individual decision process—that's it. They have no control over other participants' decision-making processes or how a number of uncontrollable variables will interact to produce a final outcome. It's like playing blackjack. A player cannot control what card is turned over next. No one knows what the next card is. No one has control over the other players' abilities to make the proper hit-or-stay decisions. The only control a player has is over her own decision process and how she wants to play the game to improve her odds of winning. Driving is a gamble and we want to stack the odds in favor of success and safety as best we can for the younger driver.

An infinite number of variables are in a constant state of flux and at any moment can cause a dangerous situation to materialize for a driver. For any driving trip, there is a driver, a vehicle, the driving environment, and driving activities that take place. Any given situation is affected by these four elements. Different situations force a driver to make numerous decisions, adjustments, and alterations. There is a direct correlation between a driver's awareness level of their surroundings and their degree of safety. The higher their situational awareness, the more safely they will operate the vehicle, process data, and make decisions given the interaction of these elements.

Table 5.1   Four Elements of Driver Safety

Driver	Vehicle	Environment	Activity
Inexperience	Sports power	Poor weather	Speeding
Stress	Poor maintenance	Other drivers	Towing a trailer
Alcohol/Drugs	Unfamiliar to driver	Road conditions	Full passenger load
Drowsiness	Improperly equipped	Traffic factors	
Peer pressure			

This is why flight instructors impress upon their students the importance of thinking at least two steps ahead and being constantly aware of situation and location while proactively looking for and anticipating problems. Good pilots and good drivers can perform all these and other tasks almost simultaneously by momentarily processing each task independently before quickly switching to the next task.

Decision Making While Driving

In the conventional decision-making process, the need for a decision is usually initiated by the recognition that something has either changed or that an expected change did not occur. The commencement of the decision-making process happens only after an event occurred or an anticipated event failed to happen. The problem is, when driving and traveling at some rate of speed, this is usually about the same time corrective action is needed. Very little time is available from recognition to resolution. You can see why decision compression is a big factor for drivers, yet many have not even heard the term. Conventional decision making applied to drivers behind the wheel of a car is inadequate in identifying and processing the specific needs brought about by compounding events and decision compression.

The aviation community recognized the inadequacy of the conventional decision-making process and realized there was room for improvement when it came to speed and accuracy in making decisions. This is not surprising considering the high number of pilot errors. In an attempt to help pilots handle the many variables associated with making complex decisions at high speeds, affecting the lives of many, the General Aviation Manufacturer's Association, FAA, and other organizations have conducted several studies concerning the decision-making process. From these efforts, the practice of aeronautical decision making (ADM) was born. ADM tweaks the conventional decision-making process to give pilots two things of which they can always use more:

1. The ability to proactively search for, analyze, and establish the relevance of all surrounding variables that might impact an upcoming event requiring a decision
2. The authority to execute and the motivation to choose a course of action within a shorter time frame (relative to everyday conventional decision making)

The decision-making process can be extremely complex and has an infinite number of input variables and outcome results. However, it can be distilled into six key elements. The aviation community uses the acronym "DECIDE." This is taught to student pilots and continuously reinforced through the pilot ranks. This acronym can be reworded for drivers to help improve their decision-making routines:

> **D**etect the fact that a change has occurred or needs to occur
> **E**stimate the need to counter or react to the change
> **C**hoose a desirable outcome for the success of the driver
> **I**dentify necessary actions that could successfully control the change
> **D**o the necessary action to adapt to the change
> **E**valuate the effect of the action

The DECIDE model adds some structure to the decision-making process. I wish to expand on and emphasize the importance of the initial detect stage. Yes, detection is critical but if one can also start to anticipate, expect the unexpected, and think two steps ahead, she should be able to increase her speed of detection and perhaps realize an event is about to happen prior to it actually happening. This will, in effect, provide more decision making and reaction time in order to take appropriate action. This tiny amount of additional time could make the difference in avoiding an accident.

When I started to train for my instrument rating, I quickly learned that things in the cockpit happen very quickly and with great complexity, making for an increase in the potential for making mistakes. Instrument flying can be demanding and impose an extremely high task load on flight crews, let alone a single pilot operating an aircraft. When the weather is bad with low visibility, pilots cannot rely on their ability to control the flight of an airplane by looking at the ground like they can in good weather. They are forced to control the flight solely by looking at their cockpit instruments. This is classified as Instrument Flight Rules (IFR). IFR is demanding and it often happens in less than ideal weather conditions. In addition, speed, balance, and G-forces create physiological conditions that trick the human brain into thinking an aircraft is in a certain controllable flight attitude or position when, in fact, it is not.

Flying IFR requires a high level of training and understanding. In fact, the instrument rating is a separate curriculum above and beyond a private pilot license. Pilots may elect to train for an instrument rating in order to be legally qualified to command an aircraft solely by instrument reference. Instrument landing approaches are demanding and require the highest degree of concentration possible. Often during instrument approaches, pilots are not only managing and controlling the aircraft by reference to instruments, but are dealing with multiple external factors as well, such as turbulence, limited outside visibility, and air traffic control instructions. One of the tricks I have picked up over my more than twenty-five years of flying is relevant to this discussion. When flying, especially when flying IFR and executing an instrument landing approach, I try to continuously ask myself two questions over and over and over:

1. "What are the two things I need to do to prepare for the next event?" Think two steps ahead.
2. "What is going to surprise me next?" Anticipate.

I think these two questions are critical to increasing the safety level of a flight (or a drive). Continually asking these two questions builds a prediction model for what might surprise the pilot or driver next. These questions have saved me many times from making careless mistakes and answering them usually improves my reaction time because I am anticipating an event and can be better prepared to handle the event once it actually does happen.

A driver who can get into the habit of continually asking, "What are the two things I need to do to prepare for the next event?" and "What is going to surprise me next?"—especially when dealing with heavy traffic, intersections, poor weather, or aggressive drivers—should react more quickly and make better decisions.

Decision Making Prior to Driving

People say the first critical decision a pilot makes regarding a flight is whether to even get into the plane and fly. Likewise, there are times when drivers need to make the decision about whether or not they should even get behind the wheel and attempt to drive. This, of course, falls into the first or personal POP zone defense because the driver has full control over the decision to drive.

Again, in an attempt to improve safety and help with decision making, pilots have a personal checklist they should quickly go through before attempting a flight. This checklist is in the form of an acronym called "IM SAFE," and it is used to help evaluate the critical factors involved in being responsible and capable of meeting the demands of managing an aircraft in flight. It also is a great tool for making the first decision—that first critical decision to even attempt to fly.

Drivers can quickly go over the IM SAFE checklist questions to identify possible causes of decreased driving performance and distractions. They are:

Illness. Do I have a fever, nausea, or other symptoms that might impair my judgment or hinder my performance?

Medication. Do I currently have any prescribed medication and/or over-the-counter drugs like antihistamines or cough suppressants in my body?

Stress. Am I currently experiencing an unusual amount of stress from home, work, or my relationships? In addition, being late for an appointment and being forced to hurry will add additional stress. Do I have get-there-itis?

Alcohol. Have I consumed any alcohol (or medication or illegal drugs)?

Fatigue. Am I fatigued or tired? This might not be significant for running to the corner store, but this should raise a caution flag if attempting a three-hour drive at night on secluded roadways.

Emotion. Am I angry, upset, or heavily preoccupied with other thoughts?

Pilots and drivers alike have "good days" and "bad days" when it comes to operating an aircraft or car. This checklist draws attention to certain factors that can impede the decision-making process, especially under the effects of decision compression. The real power of this check-list comes when a driver answers "yes" to one or a few of the questions. There is a synergistic effect with these situations so having answered "yes" to multiple questions means these elements may interact in a stronger way than if just one of the compromising factors is present. The power of this quick exercise is to simply draw attention to the driver for whom, on this particular trip at this particular time, certain variables may hinder the decision-making process, concentration level, or physical ability to control the vehicle. It helps to really take a moment to evaluate one's personal POP zone and think about how one wants to proceed.

Attitudes and Decision Making

A pilot's attitude has an impact on his or her decision-making process, which can lead to the execution of both good and poor decisions.

Having an improper attitude can impair or distort the decision-making process. Whether deciding to attempt a driving trip or having to make an immediate decision while driving, personal attitude can impede one's decision-making process. There are five hazardous attitudes that have been identified for pilots. These problematic attitudes are antiauthority, impulsivity, invulnerability, macho, and resignation. These attitudes are pointed out to student pilots and are continuously reviewed. They can be redefined for drivers as follows:

1. **Antiauthority.** *"Don't tell me."* Drivers with this attitude will likely not want to be told what to do by other drivers, road signs, or even traffic laws. They regard rules, regulations, and procedures as unnecessary—they are not applicable to an antiauthority driver. These are usually aggressive drivers.
2. **Impulsivity.** *"Do something and quickly."* This is a trait of people who frequently feel the need to do something, anything, quickly just for the sake of taking action. These drivers lack the discipline to methodically think through a possible situation and make a good decision. For them, properly thinking through an event and its outcomes takes time that they do not want to spend.
3. **Invulnerability.** *"It won't happen to me."* Drivers with this hazardous attitude feel that accidents will not happen to them because they are magically invulnerable to harm. This attitude is common in newer and younger inexperienced drivers because

they have a false sense of security and as studies have confirmed, usually overestimate their competency.

4. **Macho.** *"I can do it."* These drivers are always trying to prove that they are better than everyone else and often take risks to prove it. They are usually aggressive drivers.

5. **Resignation.** *"What's the use?"* These drivers do not see themselves as having any significant input into what happens with their lives, much less input into a decision outcome. They usually feel that when things are good, they are experiencing good luck and when things are not, they are experiencing bad luck. They go with the flow and do not show much leadership or responsibility when driving.

Having any one or a combination of these attitudes can adversely affect the aeronautical decision-making process. Drivers should be aware of these same five attitudes to better understand decision biases they might have while attempting to make driving decisions.

All drivers have some of these hazardous attitudes at one time or another depending on their mood and situation on a given day. Invulnerability is a significant mindset for young drivers to recognize because there is a tendency for younger people who have not yet had the experience of a tragic event or accident to realize that no person is invulnerable to tragedy. External factors invoke a hazardous attitude in drivers who are otherwise responsible and considerate. A breakup with a significant other, a poor report card, a denied scholarship, and peer pressure are all factors that may jump-start a dangerous and hazardous driving attitude in a young driver who for the most part drives with a good attitude.

In response to helping pilots combat and manage each of the five hazardous attitudes, antidotes were identified. Pilots are trained to recognize the onset of these attitudes and then think about and apply the appropriate antidote. Drivers who can recognize the onset of a particular hazardous attitude can also apply the corresponding antidote in an attempt to make better decisions.

Table 5.2   The Five Hazardous Attitudes

Hazardous Attitude	Antidote
Antiauthority: "Don't tell me!"	"Follow the rules. They are usually correct."
Impulsivity: "Do something–quickly!"	"Not so fast. Think it through first."
Invulnerability: "It won't happen to me!"	"It could happen to me."
Macho: "I can do it!"	"Taking chances is risky and foolish."
Resignation: "What's the use?"	"I can make a difference. My input matters."

Having these attitudes can increase the likelihood of a poor decision or a slow decision, which can then lead to an accident. No one is safe and even the most responsible drivers can be victimized by other unsafe and irresponsible drivers. Eighty percent of fatal driving accidents are attributed to error in judgment. It is important for young drivers to learn how to recognize the onset of these hazardous attitudes and how to quickly nullify them with the appropriate antidote behavior.

Stressors and Decision Making

As it relates to driving, stress can impede a driver's performance and slow reaction time. Physical, psychological, and physiological stress can affect a driver's ability to safely perform and can increase the likelihood of making a poor decision.

1. **Physical Stress.** Environmental conditions such as temperature, weather, road conditions, noise, and so forth contribute to physical stress.
2. **Psychological Stress.** Factors such as issues with family, school, friends, work, and the like can contribute to the emotional and social aspects of psychological stress.
3. **Physiological Stress.** Conditions such as fatigue, illness, and hunger, which can affect blood sugar and/or blood pressure, can all lead to physiological stress.

Any threat to the body's equilibrium causes the body to shift its resources to cope with it. Stress can cause varying combinations of reactions such as the release of chemical hormones (adrenalin), increased metabolism, and changes in heart rate, blood pressure, respiration, and perspiration. A driver's body reacting to these sources of stress and being preoccupied with thinking about the sources causing the stress diverts attention away from driving and making accurate decisions.

Task load is the number of tasks or jobs a pilot or driver is forced to manage and perform. Each person has varying levels of task loads that they can manage effectively. It is important to recognize that an individual's task-load ability changes depending on the different levels of physical, psychological, and physiological stress. I believe this is a point that young drivers need to fully understand. Just because one day you were calm and successfully managed a difficult or challenging decision does not by any means guarantee the same results on a different day with different circumstances. Changes occur and experience will teach everyone, but for the young driver who lacks both a knowledge base and decision compression experience in making rapid decisions, an understanding that skills and stress are in a constant state of flux is often lacking.

Every driver has the task of managing the safe control of themselves, vehicle, passengers, and other surrounding drivers and property. This responsibility is made more difficult by other tasks such as talking to passengers, dialing or talking on a cell phone, or changing radio stations. The level of difficulty is increased still further by adding another driver's approach, bad weather, a busy intersection, or congested traffic. With all of these issues, a driver may start to reach his personal saturation point. With distractions and tasks ever changing in intensity and duration, a driver's ability to handle stress can differ greatly at any given time on any given day. It is difficult to always know where the point of task saturation which may lead to bad decisions is at any given moment.

Once again competency silos are relevant here, as they allow for drivers to falsely generalize that they are competent to manage certain driving situations because they managed similar situations in the past. The variables, attitudes, and stress factors are most likely different from those experiences in past driving situations. Everything changes and each driving situation needs to be evaluated and processed separately. It is a great idea to draw from previous experiences to help make the best decision for a given situation, but do not fall into the competency silo trap by simply taking the solution from your "intersection management" competency silo and duplicating it for the current situation without making adjustments for the different variables in play.

Task Saturation

There will come a point where the driver's ability to manage his task load approaches a saturation point. As the task load increases, the driver no longer has the ability to rationally manage the task load. He fails to keep up with the urgent demand to make one fast decision after another, often with only a second or two to make all of the decisions. Stress will exponentially increase and panic will most likely ensue.

Drivers who all of a sudden have a spike in their task load with a reduced amount of time to deal with these tasks instantly find themselves caught in the decision compression chamber. Stress and panic have a big effect on the decision-making process and thus the combined combination of task saturation and stress can cause a breakdown in the ability to effectively process information and make good driving decisions.

Attitude Adjustments

My preflight preparation ritual has many components that are necessary before a flight: I plot my intended course, obtain a detailed weather briefing, calculate many factors such as fuel consumption and the distance to alternate airports, and preset my instruments and radios for the first phase of flight. Once everything is ready to go and prior to starting the engines, I take a few moments to reset my attitude to one that is conducive to flying. I take a few deep breaths and remind myself that I am now commencing an event for which I have a strong passion, yet it is dangerous, full of challenges, and unexpected surprises. The goal is to keep my cool and make reasonable and sound judgments—perhaps hundreds of them during one flight. I also remind myself that although I do, in fact, enjoy thrill-seeking events and crave the need to "live on the edge" once in a while, driving and flying are two activities where pushing the edge with risky behavior is not appropriate for me, my family, my passengers or the innocent people sharing the road or air with me.

I recommend that all drivers, especially younger drivers, take a few moments to reset their attitudes prior to driving a vehicle. They should remind themselves of the same thing: There is a time and place for thrill seeking and living on the edge, but driving is not one of those places. They should quickly run through the IM SAFE checklist and make a quick mental evaluation to see if one or more of the five hazardous attitudes are present. A "yes" to one or more of these checklist items does not necessarily mean that one must cancel the trip, it merely highlights a caution area for which the individual needs to pay close attention.

Review

- Teenage drivers are thrown into challenging situations in which they have to make fast and accurate decisions under pressure. This occurs even though most teenagers have limited driving experience and little to no previous experience in making critical split-second decisions while under decision compression.
- Decision compression often forces a driver into task overload and panic when the sudden onset of dangerous circumstances

occurs. Panic typically causes slower reaction and decision times and this often causes the driver to second guess their first reaction further compounding panic.

- Anticipating and thinking two steps ahead will help identify dangerous situations sooner, giving the driver additional time in which to make decisions.
- Drivers should become familiar with the pilot's DECIDE decision model. It helps educate pilots in making safer decisions under pressure and can help a driver also make safer decisions.
- Drivers should quickly go through the IM SAFE checklist to help highlight potential issues prior to each driving trip or before riding as a passenger.
- Drivers should make a commitment to always make decisions that err to conservative.
- Pilot habits that apply to drivers' decision making are anticipation, erring to conservative, having situational awareness, and breaking the trend.

Chapter 6
Speeding

Ah, yes, the need for speed. The pilot in me cannot get enough of it. I love flying fast and the challenge that speed brings. It is a strange feeling to go from flying at 540 miles per hour to getting in the car and driving home with a top limit of 55 or 65 miles per hour—but speed is a relative thing. Although I guess driving the speed limit surrounded by other drivers, some of them careless, some of them tailgating, and some of them drunk or high is also challenging.

Speed variance is the leading cause of speed-related crashes. Variance relates to multiple motor vehicles all sharing a lane or adjacent lanes traveling at different speeds. This variance in speed means the faster-moving vehicles usually want to pass the relatively slower-moving vehicles. These impatient drivers are concerned with keeping their pace and not slowing down, thus resulting in a higher activity of lane cutting and lane changing in and out of slower-moving traffic. In areas that have vehicles driving at different speeds, the likelihood of accidents increases.

Speed has a direct impact on a driver's decision-making process and reaction time and these in turn have a direct impact on the decision compression model. As a vehicle's speed increases, it covers more distance in a given amount of time. And then the faster it moves, the less time a driver has to recognize and react to a situation before physically encountering that situation. It's the old $d = rt$ equation; distance = rate × time. However, we will examine the many variables that affect just how fast things happen when driving along the road. Manipulating these variables can add that precious second or two of additional reaction time.

Stopping Distance

There are four factors that determine a driver's ability to stop a vehicle:

1. **Perception distance.** The distance a vehicle travels from the point in time the driver sees a pending event until the brain rec-

ognizes and confirms that it is an event requiring a decision and subsequent reaction.

2. **Processing distance.** The additional distance a vehicle continues to travel while the brain processes input information, contemplates alternatives, and then finally decides on the best course of corrective action to take.

3. **Reaction distance.** The additional distance a vehicle travels once a decision is made, the brain executes instructions, and body parts physically move to carry out the instructions. For example, the elapsed time from the brain instructing to moving the foot off of the accelerator pedal and depressing the brake pedal is reaction time.

4. **Braking distance.** The additional distance it takes to stop a moving vehicle once the brakes are applied. The distance will vary greatly depending on road conditions (dry, wet, ice), tire inflation, tire tread degradation, and the slope of the road (downhill slope increases stopping distance while uphill slope decreases stopping distance).

Many drivers assume that there is a linear relationship between speed and braking distance. I interviewed several people who erroneously believed that doubling the speed of travel only doubles the required braking distance. This defines a linear relationship and is incorrect. This is an important point to clarify. Braking distance is, in fact, proportional to the square of a vehicle's speed. This means that the braking distance increases exponentially as the speed increases. A general rule of thumb is that for every time a vehicle's speed is doubled, braking distance is quadrupled.

Let's say a mechanically sound car is traveling at 55 miles per hour along a dry road surface. Say the driver encounters a situation requiring an immediate stop. This will lock up the brakes, bringing the vehicle to a screeching halt. But first the driver will have to perceive, process, and react. And then wait until the car comes to a stop. The average driver under average conditions traveling at 55 miles per hour would most likely consume about seven seconds of time while consuming 492 feet of road from the time a potential problem was perceived until the vehicle was stopped.

An example of how the four stopping distance variables affect time and distance once a potential problem requiring action is perceived is shown in the following table.[1]

Table 6.1   Stopping Distance

Event: Distance	Average Time (in seconds)	Distance Traveled (in feet)	Cumulative Time (in seconds)
Perception	.75	60	.75
Processing	1.0[a]	80	1.75
Reaction	.75	60	2.5
Braking	4.5[b]	292[c]	7.0
Total	7.0	492 feet	

[a] A pure gut reactive response of slamming on the brakes has a processing time we will call close to 0 while a more complex decision could burn up 2 seconds or more. For this example, we split the difference and use a processing time of 1 second.

[b] Assuming a car is traveling at 55 miles per hour, a braking distance of 170 feet can be used with an associated elapsed time of 4.5 seconds.

[c] Assuming normal road conditions. Distance will increase due to wet road conditions, ice, improper tire inflation, or tire tread degradation.

The average passenger car is about 13 feet in length. If we painted a long line along a highway marking the total 492 feet of stopping distance needed in the example above, we could line up 38 average cars parked bumper to bumper. The skills of a newly licensed driver will most likely be a bit inferior to the average driver's performance, making for a longer response time than that in our example.

This is compelling information. If young drivers can begin utilizing anticipation to improve their decision-making process and thus subsequently reduce perception, processing, and reaction times by even a fraction of a second, a collision might be avoided. If by using PilotDriver skills a driver can make even a 20 percent improvement in just one of these variables, let alone an improvement in all three, the math from the above example supports that they will receive the gift of at least a car's length of stopping distance.

This is a great example of why even a fraction of a second can easily mean the difference between having or avoiding a collision. Factors such as alcohol, drugs, distractions, and the like that impede fast decision-making capabilities often add multiple car lengths to the stopping distance. The mindset I like the younger driver to consider is that of doing everything possible to get that extra car length's advantage to a shorter stopping distance. One extra car length helps to increase the driver and passenger's odds of avoiding a collision. The last car length of stopping distance is significant because that is the car length that may avoid contact.

Viewing police chase videos of fleeing cars during a pursuit, it is documented that speeds can exceed 110 miles per hour (double the 55 miles per hour used in the previous calculations). We know that the relationship between speed and braking distance is not linear. Double the speed means quadruple the braking distance so traveling at 110 miles per hour (55 miles per hour × 2) would require a minimum of 1,168 feet (292 feet × 4) to stop! That is close to the length of four football fields.

Let's say our driver going at 55 miles per hour does, in fact, see an upcoming potential hazard and needs to make a decision about what to do. The hazard to avoid is a moving car coming head on at the same rate of 55 miles per hour in this scenario, our driver has only 246 feet (half of 492 feet) because the opposing car is inbound and head on at the same speed. This, of course, assumes a best-case scenario in that both drivers immediately see the situation and react and that both cars have equal stopping capability.

As speed increases, it becomes more difficult to maneuver with control inputs. When driving around a curve in the road, a force is applied (turning the steering wheel which then turns the tires) which influences the vehicle to change from its "undisturbed straight line" of moving ahead. The force between the tires and the road increases as speed and turn radius are increased (force = mass × velocity^2 divided by the turn's radius) and this increases the probability of skidding.

While turning, a higher speed increases the likelihood of driver error due to:

1. Under steering a turn.
2. Over steering a turn.
3. Overcorrecting a recovery from slipping off the edge of the road. This particular situation arises from under steering the turn at the start.

Australia's University of Adelaide National Health Medical Research Council (NHMRC) Road Accident Research Unit completed an interesting study that quantified the relationship between driving speed and the probability of being involved in a fatal crash. The theory for the study is that a baseline be established for sober drivers that the risk of being in a fatal crash is relatively low. From this baseline, certain events like speeding raise the likelihood of a fatal crash significantly.

The main objective of the study was to determine and measure speed's risk for sober drivers traveling at 60 kilometers per hour (37.28 miles per hour, rounded to 37 miles per hour). The study concluded that 68 percent of fatal crashes occurred above 37 miles per hour. Results documented that the risk of involvement in a fatal crash for a car traveling over 37 miles per hour increased at an exponential rate. For every 3.11 miles per hour (5 kilometers per hour) over 37 miles per hour, the odds of being in a fatal crash double. The risk of involvement in a fatal crash are twice as likely when traveling at 40 miles per hour as they are at 37 miles per hour, four times as likely when traveling at 43 miles per hour, and so on.

This study highlights the need for vigilance in seeing and avoiding speeding drivers. This is a significant exponential relationship and it applies to sober drivers. Imagine how the odds jump when combining a speeding driver who has been drinking or is under the influence of some substance other than alcohol. Drivers greatly exceeding the speed limit are already exhibiting risky behavior. Chances are they will operate recklessly and weave in and out of traffic and cut other drivers off. They manufacture multiple opportunities for losing control of their vehicle and/or causing other drivers to have to make evasive maneuvers which, in turn, may cause a ripple effect that jeopardizes yet more drivers trying to share the same road space.

Speed and DUI

In 2001, excessive speed was a contributing factor in over 30 percent of all fatal crashes, resulting in 12,850 lost lives.[2] How many of these lives belonged to irresponsible adults with multiple previous DUI convictions driving on a suspended license? How many were newly licensed teenage drivers being responsible and trying to make the right choices to stay safe but just happened to be in the wrong place at the wrong time and got torpedoed by a speeding drunk? How many were children in a car seat rammed from the side by a reckless driver running a red light? These are questions for parents and their younger drivers to ponder together.

I remember from my Emergency Medical Technician and rescue squad experience that it often seemed to be the innocent or non-drinking party of an accident that was more seriously injured. I remember thinking several times how unfair it was to see the drunk driver upset about his or her car being damaged while I attended to the family members they crashed into.

Speed and alcohol are a deadly combination. In 2001, 39 percent of all drivers with a blood alcohol content (BAC) of 0.08 or higher involved in fatal crashes were speeding, compared to only 14 percent of sober drivers. For drivers under the age of 21, 29 percent of speeding drivers involved in fatal crashes had a BAC of 0.08 or higher. In contrast, only 12 percent of the non-speeding drivers had a BAC of 0.08 or higher.[3]

Looking at the next older age group, drivers between the ages of 21 and 24, who were involved in fatal crashes in 2001, a staggering 51 percent of speeding drivers were intoxicated.[4] This means more than half of the drivers in fatal accidents in this age group were not only drunk but were also speeding. Perhaps this increase is partly due to the fact that people can legally buy alcohol at this age, making it much more accessible. In addition, I have to believe that inexperience—or maybe a better word is irresponsibility—also plays a role. Once again, events quickly interact and compound together: inexperience, alcohol, excessive speed, and no safety belts. Sprinkle in a dash of peer pressure and a smidgen of being unfamiliar with the roads and the recipe for a tragic event is complete.

Speed and Night Driving

During darkness, conventional head lamps from an average vehicle can illuminate the road in front of it to a distance of about 160 feet with low-beam lighting. The distance may increase up to 300 feet with high-beam illumination.

Notice that even in ideal situations with correctly operating equipment and tires, stopping distance exceeds the forward illuminated roadway at speeds between just 35 and 40 miles per hour. Above this speed, a car will be overdriving the illuminated road surface ahead. Given low-beam headlight illumination, when driving at speeds above 40 miles per hour there is not adequate stopping distance once an obstruction is clearly identified in the light beam. In addition, if high-beam illumination is used, overdriving forward illumination will occur at speeds of about 55 miles per hour. Therefore, at night, at speeds in excess of 55 miles per hour, and using high-beam headlights, these figures indicate that drivers will not have enough time to detect a situation, process a potential threat, react, and stop. Do you drive over 55 miles per hour at night with your high beams on?

What is more significant is that these figures are for "normal" driving conditions. Headlight illumination cannot follow a bend in a road or track the ups and downs of a hill, which further shorten forward illumination. Fog, precipitation, drowsiness, and medications further jeopardize one's ability to react in a timely fashion. Add alcohol into this mix to further slow detection, processing, and reaction times and the chances for an accident increase even further. Add in the attributes of a typical teen driver—inexperienced, distracted, and prone to peer pressure—to further compound the situation, a situation in which we are still just talking about vehicles traveling in the 40 to 55 miles per hour range. A speeding driver will certainly be outside of the safe stopping envelope at night.

Incidentally, the National Highway Traffic Safety Institute Administration reported in 2001 that between the hours of midnight and 3 A.M., 78 percent of speeding drivers involved in fatal crashes had been drinking.[5] This is yet another staggering statistic proving the need for nighttime vigilance. Anticipate, expect the unexpected, and see and avoid.

Speed and Impatience

When hurrying to get to a destination more quickly, increasing speed, passing other vehicles, or reckless driving may cut a few moments off of a driving trip but at what cost? For example, say a driver has 5.1 miles left to go to complete her trip home. She decides to make an aggressive pass around a driver traveling at the 50 miles per hour speed limit. To execute the pass, the impatient driver increases her speed to 60 miles per hour and consumes one-tenth of a mile to complete the pass. During this tenth-of-a-mile pass, the increase in speed cuts a mere 1.2 seconds off of her drive time home. Then for the remaining 5 miles the driver cuts off an additional 1 minute of driving time, making a total time savings of 61.2 seconds. So theoretically yes, the impatient driver has accomplished her objective of speeding up to reduce travel time.

However, we have learned that for every 3.11 miles per hour speed increases above 37 miles per hour, the odds of being in a fatal crash double. In this example, the driver went 10 miles per hour faster, or roughly 3 times the 3.11 miles per hour increase. Braking distance increases exponentially as speed increases. With the impatient driver now moving 20 percent faster (from 50 miles per hour to 60 miles per hour), perception, processing, reaction, and braking distances will be elongated. Decisions will have to be made more quickly. If an incident were to happen while passing the slower vehicle, then that driver could be forced to take corrective action that is outside of her ability.

The point of this example is to be aware of the risk associated with increased speed and other associated increased risky behaviors. There is a synergistic relationship and an exponential increase in risk given a fairly minor increase in time savings. At the end of this trip home, the driver only saved about 1 minute of driving time and greatly increased her odds of being in an accident. Chances are that she would have been stopped by a red light or found herself behind another slower driver and might not have saved any time at all while still increasing her risk substantially.

Review

- Breaking distance exponentially increases with speed. As a general rule, braking distance quadruples every time speed is doubled.
- Chances of a fatal crash increase exponentially with speed. The chances of being involved in a fatal crash continuously double for every three miles per hour increase in speed over 37 miles per hour.
- Several factors like weather, road surface conditions, tire conditions, and road grade cause stopping distances to vary.
- The average driver overdrives their low-beam headlight illumination once speed exceeds 40 miles per hour and high-beam headlight illumination once speed surpasses approximately 55 miles per hour.
- Traveling at faster rates of speed directly reduces reaction time, further exacerbating decision compression.
- Traveling at high speeds causes drivers to overcorrect when recovering from turning errors.
- Pilot habits that apply to speeding are anticipation, awareness of compounding events, thinking two steps ahead, seeing and avoiding, and breaking the trend.

Chapter 7
Intersections

The U.S. Department of Transportation's Federal Highway Commission reports that 2.8 million intersection–related crashes occurred in the year 2000, representing 44 percent of all reported crashes. In addition, approximately 8,500 fatalities (23 percent of total fatalities) and almost 1 million injury crashes (48 percent of all injury crashes) occurred at or within an intersection area.

Driving along a highway is like cruising during the enroute phase of a flight; for the most part, both are routine and uneventful. Conversely, I equate driving through an intersection or in traffic congestion like flying that 10 percent of a flight that includes the takeoff/climb and approach/landing. It is this relatively small portion of the flight that causes 71 percent of aviation accidents. Similar to the dynamics of taking off and landing, there is a great deal happening in an intersection. The dynamics for decision compression and task saturation can quickly catch even a safe driver off guard.

Intersections can be as simple as one side street intersecting another, or extremely complex with multiple roads, turning lanes, traffic lights, and heavy traffic. Several variables like signals, pedestrians, and cross traffic, along with other drivers trying to make it through the intersection, will present challenges for any driver. Intersections present an environment where several variables interact and situations can develop quickly. There are several different decision forces behind the activities like traffic light changes and the decisions other drivers make while entering and leaving the intersection. Intersections are a strong breeding ground for serious decision compression challenges and accidents.

A simple scenario might be you are the only vehicle on the road and you are approaching a traffic light that just turned yellow. You quickly contemplate your options and decide you should stop for this light because it will most likely turn red by the time you get there. Contemplation usually indicates that an err-to-conservative decision is warranted. This is a simple event because there is one decision (you deciding to proceed through the yellow traffic light or stop for the pending red light) and there is one decision maker—you. You are the single force making the decision. This is a personal POP zone event because you have direct control over the outcome.

More often than not, though, a few less severe mistakes, made back to back, can build into a serious situation. These compounding events usually occur quickly and by the time an inexperienced driver realizes it is happening, he has his hands full and is in need of making some fast and accurate decisions. I want to revisit our earlier discussion of how two of our five PilotDriver concepts, decision compression and compounding events, go hand in hand for pilots and have a synergistic relationship. Drivers negotiating intersections will often find similar situations.

An example of compounding events might be a pilot flying along and realizing that there is severe weather ahead. The pilot starts to consider turning left to avoid the bad weather when the air traffic controller asks her to make a turn to the right to avoid another airplane in the vicinity. Immediately after that comment, the engine begins to run rough and the pilot is sure an engine malfunction now exists.

It was no problem for the pilot to decide to turn left to avoid the upcoming bad weather. However, now there is a compounding problem in that the pilot wanted to turn left, air traffic control said to turn right, there is another aircraft nearby, severe weather ahead, and to top it all off, there is now an engine issue. She is now forced to manage compounding events and decision compression. Say this all happens within one minute and it is easy to understand that in addition to flying the plane, the pilot needs to make several complex and tough decisions that are all interrelated. At the same time the pilot is executing the emergency engine problem checklist, she must continue to control the plane while asking herself:

- Should I declare an emergency?
- Should I fly to the closer airport that is only five miles away but toward the deteriorating weather or should I try for the airport further away but located in better weather?
- Where is the plane that is in my vicinity and what are its intentions?
- Is the weather deteriorating all around me?
- Should I shut down the engine and make an emergency landing in a field?

This is a simple scenario and I use it to illustrate the process of compounding events and a new driver approaching an intersection.

There is relevance. A young driver might have to make as many critical decisions as our pilot friend in this previous scenario and may likely find himself having to make these decisions in a much faster time frame.

Instead of one to two minutes, the young driver's decision and re-action time may be compressed into maybe one or possibly two seconds while approaching an intersection where several other drivers congregate. To exponentially compound the problem further, the reactions of the other drivers in the intersection responding to the same potential threat may force the young driver to further alter his original out or force the creation of a subsequent out. This eats up precious reaction time and further compounds the decision compression squeeze and forces the younger driver closer to task saturation.

Intersections are a stage for drivers of different experience levels driving different vehicles, all with different reasons to hurry. All of this combined creates a situation in which the young driver could be forced to make a series of rapid decisions. The following four reasons are why so many young drivers get caught up in intersection accidents:

1. The average young driver does not have a significant amount of experience to draw from in reviewing alternatives in an attempt to make a "best" decision for a particular set of challenges.
2. The average young driver has little experience in processing alternatives and making split-second decisions under pressure while several events are taking place simultaneously around him or her.
3. Numerous dynamic factors simultaneously occurring are constantly changing and causing confusion in the decision-making process. Changing traffic lights, other vehicles, emergency vehicles, and the like will force the younger driver to make, then question, then perhaps change an initial decision. Second guessing an initial decision will burn up more reaction time.
4. Distractions like cell phones, a loud radio, friends, sun glare, bad weather, and so forth will add to the pressure of making a fast and accurate decision.

Some young drivers will panic when forced to make a split-second decision in this type of situation. Some will hesitate, but even the slightest hesitation will usually prove too long from which to recover. Some will make a good first decision but then other factors will force them to reconsider that first decision and react with a subsequent decision. Because we cannot instantly infuse years of driving experience and decision-making experience while under pressure into younger drivers, they need to be aware of the challenges. As parents, we need to provide tools to help them recognize and manage decision compression, task saturation, panic, and the many other associated decision-making dynamics.

"Piloting" Toward an Intersection

Fortunately, we can borrow a few procedures from flying, change them around a bit, and have a nice procedure for a young driver to use while approaching every intersection, regardless of its complexity. After some practice, younger drivers can use this sequence, or checklist if you will, to approach an intersection with confidence and awareness while already having an emergency action plan crafted and ready to execute should the light change or a driver cut in front of them.

A driver approaching an intersection, in my mind, is similar to a pilot approaching to land. To greatly simplify the process of landing an airplane, the pilot surveys the runway environment for weather, wind direction, obstacles on the runway, and other aircraft traffic. Then a checklist is gone through in order to prepare the aircraft for landing. The pilot maneuvers the airplane according to the anticipated approach. However, anything can happen at the last second such as a gust of wind, an engine problem, or even another aircraft taxiing onto the runway, to force a rapid decision, quick reaction, and a change of plan for the landing pilot.

Instead of a pilot approaching to land, a young driver approaching an intersection will benefit from this process of "CLEARing" an intersection. This process will help prepare them to anticipate what might happen and to have an action plan already in mind should the need arise for a fast decision and/or an evasive action. In effect, we are trying to do some of the work ahead of time by understanding potential threats (anticipating events) and having a plan ready to go (building outs) should the need arise. This will reduce recognition time, reaction time, and panic time.

CLEARing an Intersection

If young drivers can get into the habit of CLEARing each and every intersection on their approach to the intersection, they will have more confidence, be more alert, and will have at least one emergency out in their back pockets ready to go. This applies to all complexities of intersections.

It does not matter if the intersection is as simple as one side street intersecting another or a complicated multilane, multilight intersection. Drivers need to understand what type of intersection they are approaching and what currently is happening there, then try and quickly determine threats and be ready to react to any deviations from what is expected.

Conclude
Look
Evaluate
Apply
React

Conclude: What Type of Intersection Is It?

Each intersection is designed to operate in a certain way. As young drivers approach each and every intersection, they need to quickly determine what controls the flow of traffic and pedestrians through that intersection. Who has the right of way? Does cross traffic have to stop? Is there a side street entering onto the road? Is there merging traffic? What type of intersection traffic control is present—is it a stoplight, flashing red light, flashing caution light, or four-way stop sign?

In addition to determining the type of intersection flow control (if any), drivers need to check for other complicating factors such as:

- Railroad tracks
- Merging lanes that have a continuously green light
- Hills or curves that might make it hard to see the intersection ahead of time
- Signs or buildings restricting visibility to other traffic approaching the intersection

Look: Scan Around

Look for possible threats. Once the type of intersection traffic flow control is known and the surroundings are noted, the young driver needs to quickly build a mental list of what can happen at this intersection to pose a threat to safety. This action will become intuitive after some practice and will quickly start to occur as a process that goes automatically through the mind.

A possible threat at any intersection is that of another driver who fails to yield the right of way. This is a standing threat and is the cause of many intersection accidents. Pick any number of reasons: driving while under the influence, a malfunctioning light signal, distraction, poor weather, an attempt to stop failed as the driver slid through the intersection due to slippery roads, or perhaps they fell asleep at the wheel. You could list hundreds of excuses for a driver failing to yield to you. Expect the unexpected. Just because another driver is supposed to stop for a red light does not mean she will. Again, there are several threats at each intersection, they vary from intersection to intersection, and they include:

- Other vehicles failing to yield
- Poor road conditions
- Drunk or impaired drivers
- Emergency vehicles approaching the intersection
- Signs or buildings obstructing your view or the view of other drivers approaching the intersection
- Construction (also confusing construction signs)

Visual scanning is an important skill when flying. Whether a pilot is scanning the many instruments on the airplane's panel or scanning outside the cockpit in an attempt to locate other aircraft and landmarks, scanning skills are important, especially while flying in poor weather using only flight instruments to maintain aircraft control. When flying solely by instruments, a pilot may complete a full instrument scan in a few seconds and repeat this procedure for several hours. Needless to say, it can become extremely tiring and requires discipline and concentration.

Instrument fixation occurs when a pilot's scan is interrupted or unacceptably slow; the pilot fixates on one or a few instruments and fails to make a complete scan. An incomplete scan means critical information is not being seen or processed. Primary instrument data needs to be checked and validated against secondary instrument data to ensure all instruments are working properly. Fixation is a negative and often means that the pilot is failing to gather all relevant data.

I mention instrument fixation to show the parallel between it and a driver's attention to the roadway straight ahead of them. I believe all drivers tend to slip into that hypnotic trance many times during a driving trip and mindlessly cruise down the road. If a driver can make frequent scans to each side, then scan the side and rearview mirrors, they will greatly improve their situational awareness. This skill will be of value during the entire driving period, but it is particularly useful when approaching intersections. Proper scanning techniques are skills that most pilots develop over time.

The Scanning Driver

I believe younger drivers tend to fixate straight ahead by default and need to be taught and reminded to make complete scans while driving. We need to teach them to be cognizant of their surroundings. Now that intersection dynamics are understood, they need to perform a quick scan to determine their surroundings. Having blind spot mirrors on the rearview mirrors is an excellent way to accurately improve this scan. Through their scan, they can determine the flow of other vehicles and what vehicles are either at or approaching the intersection from different angles.

Tell new drivers to look ahead, noting the distance between them and the vehicle immediately in front (if any). They should also note any vehicles in lanes to the left and right of their current lane (if any). It is also critical that they scan the shoulders of the road on either side to note if there are any vehicles or hazards there. Finally, have them determine if any vehicle is directly to the rear and if so, how far the separation is. All of this only takes a moment. However, this helps to anticipate and think two steps ahead.

With this information, new drivers now know what they have to work with—assuming other variables remain constant. For example, because they are now anticipating a threat at an upcoming intersection, they can make plans and build outs. After completing a scan of the upcoming intersection, they know that there is a car next to them in the right lane, but there is no traffic in the left lane—the left lane is now of use. This empty left lane has just become an out. Because the left lane is clear of traffic, it is a place they can quickly move into to avoid a vehicle failing to stop at their intersection. This becomes one possible out for them to quickly execute to avoid an accident.

Drivers who can improve the visual scanning of their surroundings will increase situational awareness and will begin to improve anticipation of unexpected events which in turn lends to timely building of outs to events sooner. Through this education and consistent use of the scan, the new driver can be on the lookout for the 80 percent of drivers who are going to make a decision error, causing the approximate 1 million annual injury-producing accidents at or within an intersection area.

Evaluate: Check Your Options

Quickly evaluate your options and build your outs or escape plans based on the threats at hand. Let's say as you approach a different intersection in the left of two lanes, you note a car coming from the right crossroad that is supposed to stop for you. In addition, there is a disabled car on the right shoulder with the driver trying to fix a flat tire.

After a young driver completes his scan, he now knows there are no vehicles ahead occupying the left shoulder. Therefore, using the left shoulder has just become an out to escape to should he need to avoid both threats on the right: the approaching car and the motorist changing the tire. Making a complete scan, processing threats, and building outs prior to entering an intersection gives a game plan to have ready to execute on a moment's notice.

The motorist on the right shoulder is a threat because she is changing a tire. Why is changing a tire on the shoulder of a road a threat? Do not assume that everything will proceed as it should. Instead, assume that something will always go wrong. Expect the unexpected. The motorist may trip and fall into your lane, causing him to have to swerve. She may drop the spare tire and it may roll on a collision course with his car. Remember one of the questions I repeatedly ask, especially when approaching to land my plane: "What is going to surprise me next?" Asking this question and seeing the woman lean her spare tire against the car, might prompt the driver to answer this question with, "The spare tire might roll into my path," and start to build an out. Any driver asking this question while driving, especially when entering intersections, should be better prepared to react to a surprise threat.

Apply: Visualize Your Outs

Now that he has anticipated and identified some potential threats and has built an action plan, he continues to approach the intersection, staying aware of the surroundings, and applying the outs if needed. Expect someone or something to create a dangerous situation and be ready for it.

React: Taking Safe Action

Being the astute and predictive driver he was when entering the intersection, his improved scanning has increased his situational awareness. He has identified threats by anticipating the next event to surprise him and has built an out. Should the spare tire start to roll into the road, Mr. Driver can quickly slow down and move into the left lane in an attempt to avoid it because he previously confirmed there was no driver close behind and that there were no cars in the left lane. He just executed an out he thought up while entering the intersection.

From this preplanning, he anticipated potential threats and thought about how to avoid them if they were to happen. You have, in essence, already done the hard work and completed several steps that had they not been done prior to arriving at the intersection would have taken up recognition time, reaction time, and panic time.

A Personal Example

I remember one winter day when this procedure came into play. I had flown a small single engine airplane to Erie, Pennsylvania. Winter icing presents a severe threat to pilots, especially while flying small planes that have limited equipment to combat icing. Cold temperatures and visible moisture can create an opportunity for water to freeze upon impact onto the surface structure of an aircraft. Even the slightest accumulation of ice on the wings can severely reduce an aircraft's performance and ability to fly.

I had flown from Akron, Ohio, to Erie in the morning and although the threat of icing was present, I was able to avoid the areas containing icing potential and made an uneventful flight. Upon researching the weather and making my flight plan for the return trip, the icing conditions were again favorable and chances were possible that I might encounter icing conditions. Therefore, having identified icing as one of my threats, I checked the weather again. I also obtained reports from three other pilots who had recently flown through the area. These pilots had all reported that the sky was clear above 8,000 feet and thus the threat of icing stopped once above 8,000 feet and in clear skies. Because I was flying a plane with good climbing ability and knowing that above 8,000 feet I would escape icing, I proceeded to take off for the return flight home. My identified threat was icing and my out was a fast climb to above 8,000 feet.

Sure enough, about five minutes into the flight, the aircraft started to accumulate ice on the wings and outer surfaces. I immediately activated my out, radioing air traffic control and requesting "an immediate climb to 8,000 feet to get out of icing." Without hesitation, they granted me clearance. I quickly climbed and was out of icing once I reached 8,000 feet.

I elected to make the return trip home because I had anticipated my possible threats, researched my escape options, and created an escape plan. I was expecting an icing problem and already had my escape plan in mind. Once I ran into what I had anticipated, there was no recognition time, reaction time, or panic time wasted.

There were more factors involved in making the decision to return home that day in those conditions but this illustrates the importance of anticipation and thinking two steps ahead. The fact that I had received reports from competent pilots stating that they had recently flown through that area and all had verified that the skies were clear above 8,000 feet was the key reason I felt confident I had an escape plan.

On the Road Application
This simple aircraft icing story relates a pilot's training to the younger driver. Always thinking ahead and trying to anticipate what factors will present a dangerous situation naturally leads to the creation of outs at your fingertips for immediate execution. Verifying and escaping from this icing situation probably took five to ten minutes to unfold. Approaching an intersection and encountering its potential threats could unfold in two seconds or less; this is a situation involving driver decision compression.

Therefore, always prepare for the possibility that vehicles approaching you from the side will invade your space in an intersection and create a dangerous situation for you. This is especially true if you are stopped at a red light and then it turns green. Before you automatically pull ahead on the green light, look one more time for cross traffic. I am willing to bet that this one procedure will, by itself, save you from at least one accident. Always anticipate a "red-light runner" or "stop sign runner" at every intersection. Wait until you are sure no one will run the light before pulling out.

This especially holds true when approaching an intersection when your light has just turned green because a green light for you means the signal for traffic approaching from your side has just turned red. An impatient or unaware driver may speed through the red light. Likewise be vigilant in preventing yourself from becoming a red-light crasher and threatening another driver who now has a green light. Keep aware of the color of your light as you approach the intersection. The longer the signal is green as you approach, the more likely it is to change as you get closer. A trick when approaching an intersection on a green light, when visibility is impaired by a vehicle in front you, is to look through their rear window and windshield to see the approaching traffic light. You look through their car. This will help you keep track of the traffic light color.

Running Red Lights

It is reported that over 900 people die and nearly 200,000 are injured annually in crashes resulting from drivers running red lights.[1] A study conducted by the Insurance Institute for Highway Safety in the early 1990s in urban driving areas profiled "red-light runners." As a group, red-light runners were younger, had poorer driving records, and were less likely to wear seat belts than those drivers who did not run red lights. This matches the profile of drivers with a higher propensity for risky behavior.

When approaching an intersection with traffic lights, CLEAR the intersection. Time and anticipate the light change. If it just turned green, proceed with caution. However, if it is green as you approach, be prepared for it to turn yellow and then red. You should mentally note how much time will elapse between when you first notice the light and how long it will take you to go through the intersection. Then try and determine if the chances are high the light will turn yellow as you get close.

Scan the rearview and side mirrors, especially blind spot mirrors, to confirm if you have a clear lane you can quickly move into or a shoulder you can pull onto should a vehicle move into the intersection and threaten to collide with you. Note what traffic is behind you and how close it is to the situation.

As you approach, you need to make a mental decision on when to break the trend—the trend of continuing through the intersection. This is the decision which determines at what point you will go through the light and at what point you will stop should the light turn yellow. Make this decision prior to reaching the actual intersection so if the light should turn yellow as you approach, your decision will be instantaneous. Be cautious; your go/no-go decision should err to the conservative.

As you approach the intersection, a trick is to mentally select a point where you will decide to stop should the green light turn yellow. For example, you might say to yourself at 100 feet from the intersection, "I'm stopping if I see yellow." Continuing forward, at 50 feet and with the light still green, you say to yourself, "I'm stopping if I see yellow." Then maybe at 20 feet, you say, "I am now close enough that I'm proceeding with caution and going through the light if I see yellow."

The actual distances in feet are used as an example. You do not need to guess the actual distances you are from the light. Instead, gauge safe stopping points based on your comfort level depending on your speed, stopping distance, and other possible threats you identified with the intersection.

By mentally timing the light and creating a decision point to go or not to go as you approach a light, you will already have your decision made as to what action you will take the instant you see the light change to yellow. This is thinking two steps ahead. This is helpful because prior to reaching the intersection you have already reduced (1) problem recognition time, (2) problem reaction time, and (3) problem solution time. The only thing remaining is to decide whether to execute your out, which takes only problem execution time.

It is critical to be proactive in researching the surroundings and anticipating potential problems. Having situational awareness and anticipating potential problems will force you to be more cautious, and perhaps more important, you can formulate decisions and actions before a problem is even recognized. This reduces problem recognition and reaction time.

The process of anticipating every intersection with an upcoming traffic light and its chances of turning yellow, then red, mentally prepares you to decide at what point you will either proceed through the intersection or slow down and stop for the red light. This way, the instant the light turns yellow, you have your decision made on whether to proceed or stop because you have already thought about the situation and have determined your plan.

Drivers that do not anticipate the red-light change could easily choke as a result of decision compression from entering an intersection with a changing traffic light. These drivers who fail to quickly make their go/no-go decision often fail to err to the conservative. These are the same drivers whom you need to look out for and anticipate as you approach or are stopped at an intersection. As stated before, if I am forced to quickly contemplate alternatives to a decision and I sense the onset of decision compression, I will, by default, immediately err to the conservative and choose the safest option.

The added complexity of changing traffic light signals causes many accidents, but intersections without a traffic light are still dangerous. Stop sign intersections are yet another area where vehicles cross paths and collisions occur. The same principal applies to non-traffic-light intersections. Anticipate the cross traffic will not stop and plan your out accordingly. Expect the unexpected. Perhaps a stop sign was stolen the night before or a traffic light has become inoperative.

Left Turns

Making left turns at an intersection poses a different set of problems from red lights. In addition to looking for "light crashers" coming from any direction, a driver turning left has to contend with crossing oncoming traffic while maintaining path track (staying in the appropriate lane).

Oncoming Traffic

While making a left turn, the driver needs to look for oncoming traffic in the lane being turned through. A driver must look for and estimate a gap in traffic that will allow a safe crossing. This requires not only good scanning techniques but also speed estimation.

Drivers in oncoming traffic will be traveling at different rates of speed and there will be different sizes of gaps between the vehicles. Drivers waiting in an intersection to make a left turn and for oncoming traffic to clear are vulnerable to taking a hit from a car running a red light. They are sitting ducks in the center of the intersection.

Lane Tracking

Once oncoming traffic is cleared and a crossing gap is present, a left turn can be made. A left turn usually requires a different and often wider radius than a right turn. Therefore, attention needs to be given to properly tracking within the correct lane path through the intersection.

In some states, many roads are now being painted with dashed paint lines that allow the driver to visually see the path track on the ground, permitting them to more easily stay within their lane while turning through an intersection.

Pedestrian Search

A third variable that needs to be managed whether making left or right turns is the crossing of pedestrians. Pedestrians may or may not cross in designated crosswalks. They may or may not cross at the designated crossing time. Remember: Expect the unexpected.

Attention needs to be divided between oncoming traffic, tracking the appropriate lane, watching for pedestrians, and of course, looking for red-light crashers. Remember that while turning to look for pedestrians, the front roof support structure of a car's body often block a driver's vision and create blind spots that can easily conceal a pedestrian crossing the road.

Right Turns

Making right turns in an intersection poses a different set of problems than left turns. A driver turning right must also look for pedestrians while at the same time looking for red-light crashers. However, the turning radius problem is the opposite from making the wider radius left hand turns. Drivers need to be careful to not turn too sharply and clip a sidewalk or curb. In general, left turns require a wider radius and right turns require a smaller or tighter radius.

Lane Tracking

Unlike a left turn, executing a right turn usually means not having to cross in front of oncoming traffic. Therefore, the turning radius is tighter and the turn is said to be a sharper turn.

Young drivers sometimes do not differentiate between the degrees of turning radius. The problem for right turns is not making a tight enough turn and as a result, drifting left of the desired lane and into oncoming traffic. Sometimes if the turn is made too tight, the rear wheels will run over the curb or corner where pedestrians may be standing.

Pedestrian Search

The same care needs to be taken in watching for pedestrians while making a right-hand turn as when making a left-hand turn.

Railroad Crossings

Railroad crossings are often taken for granted and their danger is underestimated. When railroad tracks cross a road or highway, they form an intersection that requires a driver to process information to make the decision to either continue over or stop before traversing the railroad tracks.

The National Transportation Safety Board reported in 1998 that of the approximate 160,000 public railroad-highway intersections only 20 percent have gates. However, nearly 50 percent of all collisions occur at crossings equipped with automatic warning devices and of those intersections, a crossing driver may still not hear the alert.[2] The National Safety Transportation Board also reported in 1998 that over 90 percent of all rail-related fatalities involved either grade crossings (surfacing material like wooden planks or rubber placed between rails to enhance automobile and pedestrian crossing) or trespassers and 60 percent of these deaths occurred at crossings without automated warning devices

Trains use a standard horn or whistle sequence to alert people that the train is approaching an intersection. The sequence is a long blast, another long blast, followed by a short blast, and concludes with a long blast (long-long-short-long).[3] Regulations require an approaching train to start making audible warning sounds with its horn beginning a quarter mile from a crossing. It must continue making the warning sounds until it occupies the intersection. However, buildings, terrain, local factory noises, a car with its windows up and stereo on, and so forth can reduce the effectiveness of these audible horn warnings. Many drivers involved in railroad accidents report not even hearing a horn until two seconds or less before impact.

Therefore, the young driver must respect a railroad crossing and take the responsibility of slowing down, listening carefully, and visually determining it is clear to cross. If a train is approaching and close to an intersection, the driver should assume she could make two very common optical illusion errors: that the train is closer than she thinks and that the train is moving faster than she thinks.

Drivers who underestimate a train's speed and position may try to speed up in an attempt to beat the train through the intersection. This leads to two fast-moving vehicles on a collision course. The accelerating car has now increased its stopping distance by speeding up and has intensified decision compression. Accelerating in an attempt to beat a train through an intersection is a bad idea because the car could actually hit the train. In fact, 24 percent of all car/train collisions occur when a vehicle slams into the side of a train.[4] An err-to-conservative decision means electing not to go and instead waiting for the train to pass. In addition, and especially with a multiple track intersection, the driver should anticipate another train on an adjacent railroad track. The driver should wait until all tracks are visible and clear before crossing after the first train passes through the intersection.

Drivers often make six common mistakes when approaching a railroad crossing. They are:

1. They fail to properly clear the intersection visually and audibly and rely solely on warning devices such as crossing gates to indicate the presence of an approaching train. These warning devices are mechanical and mechanical devices break down and fail.
2. They ignore a warning signal such as a lowered crossing gate and continue to cross the tracks.
3. They erroneously judge both how far away the train is and how quickly it is moving—especially at night.
4. They fail to realize that approaching a railroad-highway crossing that is not at a 90 degree angle further complicates accurate perception of both speed and distance.
5. They fail to re-clear the railroad crossing after a train has passed, increasing the chances of missing the presence of a pedestrian or a second train on an adjacent track.
6. They fail to realize that different parts of the human eye have to quickly alternate between interpreting and processing the information taken in when the car approaches a railroad crossing with a moving train approaching from an angle. The fovea is a small area of the eye located on the retina directly behind the lens and is where vision is the sharpest. While looking straight ahead at the intersection, an image of a large approaching train lingers in the eye's peripheral vision area, which is outside the eye's fovea. Peripheral vision only accurately sees one-tenth of what the eye can accurately see with the fovea. Using this less-accurate peripheral vision to process the side movement of a large train or quickly moving the fovea back and forth to look directly at both the intersection and approaching train can lead to visual interpretation errors. Night vision further degrades a person's ability to accurately determine movement and speed of an object. We will discuss more about vision and the human eye in the next section on night vision adaptation.

Trains are heavy and a moving train has a lot of energy and momentum behind it. The average train weighs approximately 12 million pounds, resulting in a train-to-car weight ratio of 4,000 to 1. By way of comparison, this is roughly equal to the ratio of a car to an aluminum can.[5] An average-sized train traveling at 55 miles per hour can take at least one mile to stop once the brakes are engaged. However, most collisions occur with trains traveling under 30 miles per hour.[6]

Review

- Intersections are a breeding ground for decision compression. When approaching each and every intersection, anticipate having to make defense maneuvers.
- CLEAR each intersection, paying particular attention to developing and being ready to execute an out plan.
- Always anticipate that another driver will not stop as required by a traffic signal, and will continue on a collision path with you.
- Always look one additional time to verify your path is clear after stopping at an intersection. It is especially important to look for side traffic not stopping as their light turns red and yours turns green.
- Try anticipating the timing of a light as it changes from green. Know prior to it turning yellow if you intend to go through or stop.
- Environmental factors like precipitation and poor visibility will change the dynamics of an intersection and everyone's decision-making process and accuracy.
- In an intersection, because all vehicles are participating in the same chaotic "dance," the safety of all drivers is reduced to the safety level of the least competent driver.
- Pilot habits that apply to intersections are anticipation, building outs, erring to the conservative, expecting the unexpected, proactively looking for trouble, practicing situational awareness, thinking two steps ahead, and seeing and avoiding.

Chapter 8
Night Vision Adaptation

Pilots are required to be educated and trained on how the human eye works as it detects and processes images. In addition, they are educated on the physiological changes that happen to the eye as vision transitions from daylight vision to night vision.

The human eye works very differently at night than it does during the day, with different parts of the eye picking up the processing workload as conditions change. Drivers who simply look straight ahead and directly at an object in darkness (in the same manner they would in the daylight) are likely to be missing critical information needed to make an accurate assessment of a situation.

Night Vision

The back of the human eye has two types of light-sensing nerve endings called cones and rods and they use the optic nerve to transmit messages to the brain. It is important for drivers to realize that cones and rods work differently depending on the amount of light and that they also see areas within the field of vision differently. This means that the eye processes information differently in daylight than it does in darkness.

The fovea is located directly behind the lens on the retina. Cones are concentrated here and their population decreases as they move outward from the center of the fovea. Due to this concentration of cones, the fovea allows for seeing the sharpest images and allows people with normal vision to look directly at an object in order to obtain the best image. Doing so focuses the image on the fovea.

The fovea field of view is the most accurate but it is very small, and only makes up about one degree of your overall field of view. To educate yourself on just how small one degree of your field of vision is, take a quarter and use clear tape to attach it to a window. Now, back up 4.5 feet from that quarter, cover one eye, and look at the quarter. The area of

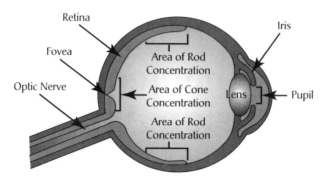

Diagram of Human Eye

your field of view covered by the quarter is approximately equal to one degree of your eye's field of view.[1] This is representative of what the fovea, capable of processing images with the highest accuracy, can see.

This is great while driving during daylight, because the fovea is best suited for seeing and making driving-related decisions when looking straight ahead. This is why drivers with normal vision tend to always look directly at objects; they are using the most accurate part of the eye to process images.

Cones

Cones allow for the detection of distant objects, detail, and color and they function both in daylight and lower light situations. However, cones become less effective as light decreases and this means that as darkness sets in, the fovea becomes less effective in processing visual information.

Rods

Rods are concentrated further out from the fovea and increase in number as the distance from the fovea increases. In daylight, rods allow for the detection of objects, particularly objects in motion as seen from the corner of the eye (known as peripheral vision). Rods do not provide detail or color, only shades of gray and motion.

As light decreases during evening hours and into darkness, the cones become less effective and a blind spot occurs; ironically, this blind spot takes over where the best vision used to be during daylight and involves an area about five to ten degrees wide in the center of the vision field. This means that off-center viewing or looking at an object slightly off center with peripheral vision often is more accurate at nighttime.

Daytime Viewing

Considering how the eye functions, the best way to view an object during the daylight is to look directly at it, keeping it in the center of the field of vision using the cone's strength of detecting color, detail, and distant objects. This is pretty cut and dry and is the normal habit of most drivers.

Nighttime Viewing

Rods work better in the darkness so the best area of vision at night is actually your peripheral vision. At nighttime, you should find that you can see objects more accurately by not looking directly at them but rather by using your peripheral vision to look five to ten degrees off the object's center. This is known as off-center viewing. Here you are forcing your brain to emphasize data from the rods (which are more accurate at nighttime and reside more in the peripheral vision) rather than the cones (which are more accurate in the daylight).

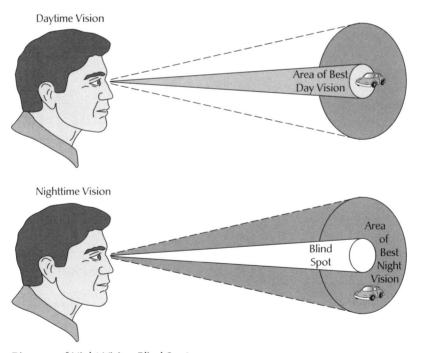

Diagram of Night Vision Blind Spot

An important point to remember about rods is that they do not detect objects well while your eye is in motion scanning the field of view. A way to improve the accuracy of night vision is to take small pauses as you look around and give the rods an opportunity to capture the data to send to the brain. This is an educational adjustment, because most drivers I studied did not know that vision worked differently at night or low light situations and continued their viewing habits of looking directly at an object during the dark hours.

While flying in darkness, pilots are taught to supplement looking straight ahead with glances of off-center viewing. It is recommended that the viewer alternate by looking straight ahead, then looking to the right for a moment and let the rods process that image. Look back to the center then glance to the left for a moment. This sequence fits well into scanning an approaching intersection.

Nighttime Transition

As nighttime sets in, many drivers continue to look directly at objects, keeping the object in the center of the same field of vision as they did during the daytime. A transition from daylight to nighttime indicates a need for a driver to transition from "cone vision" to a combination of "cone vision" and "rod vision."

An opportunity exists for safer operation in darkness if drivers supplement their habitual direct viewing with peripheral or "corner of the eye" viewing. Alternating and combining these two sources of viewing will help detect more accurate data by offsetting each others' weakness during low light situations.

Headlights

Anything you can do to promote safety, and more importantly your child's safety, is a good thing. In my opinion, headlights should be on all the time and in fact, newer model cars try to accomplish this with automatic light activation devices. These newer model cars are designed to keep the headlights on to alert other drivers of the location and direction of the vehicle.

Normal operation is to have the headlights on in the low-beam setting. Properly adjusted lights direct the beams slightly to the right of center. In addition, this setting is designed to shoot light down in front of the car and have some of the light shine along the road's surface. This, in turn, helps illuminate the road while being courteous to oncoming drivers who are trying to maintain their night-vision adaptation.

An oncoming vehicle driving with its high beams or other bright lights on may be distracting. Drivers may find it more comfortable to focus their vision down at the road while looking at the centerline or white edge line. Tracking one or both of these lines with direct vision allows peripheral vision to process the oncoming image using the rods of the eye. In this situation, the rods do what they do best in tracking a moving object (vehicle) and the cones do what they do best in looking directly at a lit object (road/road paint).

On dark roads or when seeing further in front of you is needed, switch the headlights to the high-beam setting, as this setting increases forward visibility. Less light bounces off the road surface and the energy is concentrated straight ahead. High beams are usually aimed more at the center of the road and typically one light is adjusted slightly higher than the other to light up a larger field of view in front of you.

I recommend using high beams as a default method of operation, but change to low-beam operations when there is oncoming traffic. Why risk blinding drivers coming at you and causing them to lose orientation of your vehicle?

Drivers may find high-beam operation distracting in heavy rain, snow, or fog. Even while traveling on dark country roads, high-beam operation in fog and snow usually hinders visibility. This is because fog and snow are both made up of water particles; fog is essentially extremely tiny water particles suspended in the air and snow is frozen imploded water droplets. Both will take light from headlights shooting straight ahead and reflect some of it back toward the driver. This can be distracting to a driver. Low-beam lights project a beam that is lower to the ground, reflection back to the driver is reduced. Drivers will usually have better forward visibility using low-beam operation in these conditions.

Take advantage of the rearview mirror's night settings when driving at night. Most rearview mirrors can adjust with a flip of a lever and they then appear to dim the image in the mirror. Lights of other cars are still visible in the mirror but they are not as bright, thus helping to retain the eye's night vision acclimation retention.

Shadow Detection

While driving at night it is relatively easy to see something that has a light shining on it. It is more difficult to see what is not lit. Anything that reflects or moves should immediately catch your attention so that you can quickly determine if it is a threat. Objects tht are not illuminated or do not reflect light will be far more difficult to detect.

Deer are a good example of moving objects that can quickly catch a driver's attention. If deer look into headlights, their eyes will usually reflect some light. Deer tend to travel in herds and the presence of one usually means others are near. If deer themselves are not illuminated by surrounding streetlights or car headlights, sometimes their shadows can be detected.

The detection of shadows at nighttime is an important point and is another reason why using peripheral vision or off-center viewing at night can help with the detection of movement even if the moving object is not well illuminated or reflecting light. Pedestrians, joggers, and bicycle riders alongside a road in the dark dressed in dark clothes with poor illumination are really inviting an accident to happen. Alternate glances of off-center viewing can help detect their movement and alert a driver to a potential dangerous situation ahead.

Preparing for Night Vision

Pilots use a procedure for night-vision adaptation. In general, they let their eyes fully adapt to the dark and then attempt to keep them in that adjusted condition throughout the entire flight. That is why cockpit lighting is usually very dim at nighttime and if a light is needed to read a navigation chart, for instance, a red-filtered light is used because the red tint tends to not jeopardize night-vision adaptation.

It only takes about 10 seconds for cones to adjust to daylight because cones can adapt to bright light quickly. Rods, on the other hand, can take up to 30 minutes to fully adapt to dark conditions—at which point the rods are about 100,000 times more sensitive to light than were they in a lighted area.[2]

Review

- The human eye sees differently in darkness than it does in daylight.
- Direct viewing or looking directly at an object is preferred while driving in daylight. This takes advantage of the fovea and cones.
- Incorporate indirect viewing at nighttime by focusing your vision to the side of an object, allowing your peripheral vision to

process the image. This takes advantage of rods that work best at night and reduces the chances of images being lost in the nighttime blind spot.

- It takes 30 minutes for the rods of an eye to fully adapt to night vision. Bright light will reduce this night adaptation. Street lights, headlights from other vehicles, signs, taillights, and so forth make it difficult to avoid distracting light while driving.
- Night driving increases the chances of misinterpreting an object's size, distance, speed, and motion trajectory.
- Use the rearview mirror's night settings when driving at night.
- Pilot habits that apply to vision perception are anticipation, erring to conservative, expecting the unexpected, proactively looking for trouble, having situational awareness, thinking two steps ahead, and seeing and avoiding.

Chapter 9
Driving Under the Influence (DUI)

The single most significant problem contributing to traffic-related deaths is DUI (driving under the influence of alcohol or other mind-altering substances). DUI is a problem for not only the driver who is operating a vehicle while under the influence but also for the many drivers in the vicinity of an impaired driver. Alcohol was attributed to 36.6 percent of youth traffic fatalities in 2000. The percentage is even higher, though, if considering substances other then alcohol.[1]

- Traffic accidents are the leading cause of death for younger drivers 16 to 20 years of age.[2]
- The percentage fluctuates annually but data shows that roughly 30 percent of all teenage deaths are caused by motor vehicle crashes and approximately 35 percent of these fatalities are alcohol related.[3]
- Three in every ten Americans will be involved in an alcohol-related crash at some point in their lives. Studies confirm that alcohol is directly linked to 40 to 80 percent of all teenage suicide attempts, violent crimes, and domestic disputes.[4]

For simplicity, we will define impairment as being under the influence of alcohol, illegal drugs, legal medications, or any combination thereof that hinders performance. Someone who has taken too much medication or is experiencing the effects associated with medicine offering the common warning "do not operate machinery—may cause drowsiness" may have impaired judgment and slower reaction times.

Although the data within this section focuses on illegal drug use and alcohol consumption, any individual taking legal over-the-counter or prescribed medications may experience driving impairment due to overmedicating, unfavorable drug interaction (combining medicines that should not be combined), side effects, allergic reactions, or combining medications with illegal drugs or alcohol.

- Underage drinking is national in scope and is a serious problem. Recent data reveals that 87 percent of high school students have consumed alcoholic beverages.
- It is estimated that over three million teens between the ages of 14 and 17 today are problem drinkers.
- Binge drinking by students is a common concern on many college campuses.[5]

Drinking alcohol is only one component of the driving while impaired issue. Marijuana and numerous other illicit drugs can also impair driving performance. The awareness of the effects of alcohol is perhaps more widely known because studies, historical data, and trending analysis have been used for a period of time. However, the following list highlights some troubling statistics concerning illegal drug use:

- In 2000, 54 percent of high school seniors used an illicit drug at least once.
- Past year use of illicit drugs by high school seniors increased from 31 percent in 1993 to 41 percent in 2000.
- In 2000, nearly one in 16 high school seniors (six percent) reported using marijuana daily.[6]

DUI Driver Characteristics

The BAC or blood alcohol concentration is the amount of alcohol present within the blood of a person's body. Alcohol begins to concentrate in the blood when an individual consumes even a minimal amount of alcohol. Studies show that some degree of impairment begins at any level over 0.0 BAC.

In general, a person weighing 150 pounds, drinking at a rate of 1.5 ounces of alcohol (the approximate amount found in one 12-ounce can of beer or one glass of wine) per half hour, would only need to consume three drinks to reach a BAC of nearly 0.08 percent.[7] Most states have established a BAC level of 0.08 as the minimum level to be considered as DUI.

Several factors will alter BAC for the same person on different days. Variables such as prescription medication ingestion, food intake, weight, a person's fat content, and duration of drinking all contribute to differing BAC levels and rates for a person. A person weighing 110 pounds will require less alcohol than a 150-pound person to reach illegal vehicle operation BAC levels (other factors being equal). Also, it takes less time to reach illegal BAC levels if drinking on an empty stomach.

Perhaps one of the most deadly competency silos a young driver establishes concerns drinking and driving. Once teen drivers successfully complete a driving trip after drinking or while under the influence of drugs, they might falsely deduce that they can safely drink and drive. Because they fail to fully understand the different levels of BAC impairment, the fact that several variables come into play each time they drink and drive, and the fact that they are using the consumption of alcohol to test new boundaries of freedom are all leading reasons for the unacceptably high rate of teenage driving deaths related to DUI.

It is important to note that BAC rises exponentially. As a general rule, as the BAC begins to rise, an individual will experience the following problems in decision making and vehicle control at given levels of BAC.[8]

BAC Between 0.0 and 0.03
- Decision-processing time is slowed.
- Ability to process multiple decision events is slowed.
- Ability to manage multiple tasks is slowed.

BAC Between 0.03 and 0.04
- Continuation of problems from a BAC between 0.0 and 0.03.
- Reaction time is impaired.
- Ability to respond to emergencies is impaired.

BAC Between 0.04 and 0.08
- Continuation of problems from a BAC between 0.0 and 0.04.
- Tracking is impaired. The ability to track a single object such as keeping a car centered in the appropriate lane is impaired.
- Attention is impaired. Ability to manage multiple events or decisions is impaired.
- Dividing attention between tasks becomes difficult. Dividing attention between just two tasks becomes difficult.
- Comprehension time is increased. The processing time to evaluate and decide on actions is severely lengthened.

- Vision is impaired. Night vision, clearly seeing objects, and judging speed and distance is impaired and is not fast or accurate enough to see moving vehicles.
- Coordination is impaired. Coordinating related tasks like hands (steering) and feet (braking) are impaired.

BAC over 0.08

- Continuation of problems from a BAC between 0.0 and 0.08.
- Ability to judge distance and speed is impaired.
- Maintenance of steering, braking, and lane control accuracy diminishes.
- Keeping a safe separation distance from other vehicles becomes more difficult.

Results from a Marijuana, Alcohol and Actual Driving Performance study further confirm the effects of driving with a BAC above 0.08. While participating in a controlled road test, drivers with BAC in excess of 0.08 failed to accurately judge distance, safe vehicle separation, lane tracking, and speed.[9]

The likelihood of being involved in an accident after drinking or taking drugs rises exponentially—*very* exponentially. The risk of being involved in a crash rapidly starts to increase after the first drink. Studies vary on the exact numbers, but one range has been published stating that a driver with a BAC between 0.0 and 0.06 is 2 times more likely to be involved in a crash than a sober driver. With a BAC above 0.10, a person is 400 times more likely than a sober driver to be involved in a crash.[10]

Following this data and using the average drink consumption figures for an average 150-pound person, the typical individual having just three drinks in an hour can catapult himself into being up to 400 times more likely to be involved in an accident.

Think about the power of teen drivers proactively managing their POP zone defense for drinking and driving. A teenager who elects not to drink and drive (protecting their personal zone) and elects not to ride as a passenger of a drinking driver (protecting their opportunistic zone) prevents a situation that would otherwise skyrocket their likelihood of being in an accident. A sober person who elects to ride with a drinking driver will increase their likelihood of being in an accident by 400 times!

In 1996, the National Household Survey on Drug Abuse (NHSDA) conducted 11,847 in-home personal interviews with drivers age 16 and older. The purpose of this survey was to gather data on drug use because driving under the influence of drugs is somewhat more difficult to accurately study than driving under the influence of alcohol. Data from this report attempts to illustrate the effects of being under the influence of drugs and alcohol while driving motor vehicles. Principal results from this study are as follows:

- 28 percent (46.5 million people) reported driving within two hours of alcohol or drug use
- 5 percent (9 million people) drove after drug use, with or without alcohol
- 23 percent (39 million people) drove after alcohol use only

Characteristics of Drivers Who Drive After Alcohol Use

The National Household Survey on Drug Abuse (NHSDA) found that driving after alcohol use was common among:

- Those age 21 and older. However, the numbers were still high for those under 21; nine percent of those age 16 to 18 and 15 percent of those age 19 and 20
- Males (31 percent of males versus 14 percent of females)

On the most recent occasion of driving after alcohol use (with or without drugs):

- Those age 16 to 20 were more likely than drivers 21 and older to report binge drinking, defined as consuming five or more drinks on one occasion (39 percent versus 13 percent)
- Drivers age 16 to 20 were more likely than drivers 21 and older to report they drank their first and last drink in less than one hour (30 percent versus 15 percent)
- More than one-third of drivers age 16 to 20 had an average estimated blood alcohol concentration level greater than 0.08
- Female drivers 21 and older generally had higher average BAC levels than males of the same age (48 percent of females had a BAC of 0.2 versus 32 percent of males)

Characteristics of Drivers Who Drive After Illicit Drug Use

The National Household Survey on Drug Abuse (NHSDA) also found that alcohol, marijuana, cocaine, and other inhalants are drugs commonly abused by youth. Of these and other abused drugs, marijuana abuse has provoked the most study. However, any illegal drug can jeopardize driving safety and can compound risk when taken with alcohol.

Also according to the NHSDA study, driving after drug use was more common among drivers who were:

- Young (13 percent for those age 16 to 20 versus five percent for those 21 and older)
- Male (seven percent versus four percent for females)
- Never married (11 percent versus six percent for those who were married)

Driving after drug use was more common among those who reported, in the past year, being:

- Arrested (18 percent versus four percent for those not arrested)
- On probation (22 percent versus five percent for those not on probation)

Among those who reported driving after the use of marijuana:

- 60 percent reported heavy or weekly use in the past year
- Drivers age 21 and older were more likely than drivers age 16 to 20 to report driving after using marijuana in combination with alcohol (37 percent and 24 percent)
- More than half, 56 percent, felt confident that marijuana use did not at all affect their ability to drive safely
- More than half perceived that they were no more likely to be stopped by police when driving after marijuana use than on other occasions (69 percent of those age 21 and older and 54 percent of those age 16–20)
- Driving after drug use most commonly occurred on smaller roads (55 percent) in urban areas (56 percent)

The most commonly reported reasons for driving after marijuana use were that drivers felt there was "no other way to get there [to their destination]" and that they were "not high enough to cause a crash."

After the NHSDA study, a subsequent study attempted to determine the separate and combined effects of THC, the active ingredient in marijuana, and alcohol on a driver's ability to safely perform driving functions.

In this study, titled *Marijuana, Alcohol and Actual Driving Performance,* study volunteers took doses of marijuana, alcohol, and placebos in different combinations. Driving vehicles with redundant controls and accompanied by driving instructors, the subjects were given road driving tests to evaluate such activities as car following and road tracking.

Summaries from this study show there is no doubt that the THC in marijuana, in even low to moderate doses of 100–200 µg/kg (micrograms per kilogram, a measurement of dosage) does impair a driver's cognitive and psychomotor abilities to perform safe driving behavior. Specific conclusions are:

- THC alone in 100–200 µg/kg doses impairs fundamental road-tracking ability with the degree of impairment increasing as a function of the dose
- The effects of impairment from THC alone does not rapidly diminish and may even increase for up to 2.5 hours after smoking marijuana, regardless of the THC dose
- THC in the 100–200 µg/kg dose range, in combination with alcohol sufficient for producing BAC of approximately 0.04 g/dl (grams per deciliter–a result measurement), severely impairs road-tracking ability, and the degree of impairment increases with increased levels of THC
- Both alcohol doses alone and THC doses alone significantly impaired the subject's road tracking and car following performances
- THC in combination with alcohol seriously decreases reaction time, especially reaction to the deceleration of a preceding vehicle

It can be argued that the NHSDA study has some limitations and drawbacks. First, the data for this analysis is entirely self-reported and many of the questions are open to subjective interpretation. Some of the sample sizes are small, leading to statistical precision that may be inadequate. Nonetheless, it does help to paint a picture of some of the key issues facing both drivers and passengers who share the road.

What is interesting about this data is the attitudes of the drivers. More than half of the respondents who took drugs felt that:

- Marijuana did not affect their ability to drive safely
- They were no more likely to be stopped by police after using marijuana than if they had not used it
- There was no other way to get to where they wanted to go

I believe that if these drivers who were interviewed had been educated on the concepts of decision compression and competency silos and were then asked to rate their ability to manage a crisis situation, they would answer differently—if they were being honest. With only say half a second to accurately process data and make correct decisions while under the squeeze of decision compression, these questions might have been looked at differently.

This study focused on the effects of alcohol and marijuana and shows some of the attitudes and driver performance issues associated with their consumption. Today's drivers have access to many types of illegal drugs. Many have access to substances that are not illegal but can be abused, causing impaired judgement and driving ability. Keep in mind that for the sake of discussion regarding driving performance, prescription and over-the-counter drugs can also negatively impact driver performance.

Five Young Driver DUI Traps

There are five traps that young drivers fall victim to while deciding to drive under the influence. It is usually a synergistic combination of these five traps that leads young drivers to getting behind the wheel while impaired.

Trap 1: Risky Behavior Tendencies

There are several risky behavior tendencies like speeding, showing off, and not wearing a seat belt with which young drivers have to deal with. These tendencies are always out there waiting to catch a young driver off guard. When alcohol and/or drugs come into the mix, a young driver's guard is often down and he or she becomes more susceptible to one or more of these risky driving behaviors. A teenager who never exhibited any risky behavior when sober may unknowingly engage in these activities while drinking, drunk, or high.

Trap 2: DUI Competency Silos

Teenage drivers are inexperienced. That is not a good or bad thing—just a fact. They often do not realize that driving from point A to point B requires several different driving skills and decisions. Most of the time a trip is routine and only requires basic driving and decision-making skills. The same skills that were used on most previous trips are used again in an almost automatic process. Skills like stopping at a stop sign or merging onto a highway are already routine, "mastered" skills for a new driver.

At any moment, however, a decision may be required concerning an event never before encountered. New situations are always materializing and if a driver has never experienced a particular situation before, he has no competency from which to draw knowledge. He is experiencing a new event.

Driving while impaired by alcohol and/or drugs will require a longer time to initially recognize a new event. Having to make decisions about a new event will often take more time because the alcohol and/or drugs have retarded or slowed the decision-making process. Also, because it is a new event, the driver may have a small or nonexistent set of previous experiences from which to pull knowledge. The decision process becomes even more difficult if dealing with decision compression and distractions.

The trap is that impaired drivers assume that the next driving trip will be the same as the last one and the one before that. It will be just another routine trip and they will not be forced into a position to have to make a fast decision based on a never-before-experienced situation.

Trap 3: Testing New Boundaries

Young drivers have not yet completely identified their personal boundaries. They are learning new lessons and experiencing new situations; not just driving situations but social, fun, personal, and dangerous situations. This learning process is part of normal behavior and simply a part of life. We are all learning new things and having new experiences whether we are 17 or 80 years old.

However, the new sense of freedom young drivers experience with a new drivers license, a car, and eager friends tends to enhance the desire to go out and experiment with new situations—to continually discover and then discover again where their personal boundaries are and their comfort zone ends.

Again, this is standard operating procedure for normal, well-behaved teenagers. Bringing alcohol and drugs into this scenario does two things. First, it tends to stretch one's comfort zone and second, it diminishes the importance of realizing that a zone even exists.

Trap 4: Peer Pressure

Peer pressure often increases when alcohol and drugs are involved because inhibitions are generally lowered. A person might have direct peer pressure from someone encouraging them to have another drink before driving to the next event. Or perhaps the drinking driver imposes "peer pressure" on herself because of the need to be different or perhaps to show off or go sensation seeking for self-arousal.

Trap 5: "Get-there-itis"

Get-there-itis is aviation slang for a pilot who is under pressure to get somewhere without delay. It tends to cause a pilot to overstep their comfort zone, safety zone, and may lead to making hasty or riskier decisions than when not under time pressures.

This situation applies to drivers of all ages, but younger drivers feeling the pressure to make it home by a certain time or who drive faster because they are late for an event may experience a stronger version of get-there-itis. When under pressure to be somewhere, alcohol and drugs once again lower inhibitions and increase risk taking, thus greatly increasing the likelihood of an accident.

At the risk of sounding redundant, the rules of exponentiation come back into play. Though the odds of a driver causing an accident increase when he falls into any one of these traps, and the odds increase exponentially when a driver falls into a combination of these traps. We have already discussed that braking distance increases exponentially with speed. The odds of a fatal accident double for every three miles per hour over three miles per hour. The effects of alcohol increase exponentially with consumption; the odds of crashing increase exponentially with impairment. Get the picture? Remember the pilot saying I often hear, "One problem is usually manageable but several problems will kill you." Again, compounding events yield highly exponential risks.

Driving While Impaired

There is ample research data that details the physiological and psychological changes alcohol and drugs have on the body. As important, there are also studies concluding that people react differently to drugs and alcohol under various circumstances. To summarize:

- Taking illegal drugs is prohibited.
- It is against the law for anyone under the age of 21 to consume alcohol—in any state.
- It is against the law for anyone under the age of 21 to drive after consuming any amount of alcohol. Many drivers under the

age of 21 are surprised to receive a citation for driving after having only one drink. "But I am not drunk," they tell the officer. True, their BAC was acceptable and under the legal limit of 0.08 but they forget that drinking any amount of alcohol under the age of 21 is prohibited.

- Deciding to drive while impaired is a personal or POP zone decision. It is your decision to drive or not to drive while impaired. Deciding not to ride with an impaired driver is an opportunistic POP zone decision. Both are very easy to manage but it requires good judgment and awareness to make these decisions.

Despite strong supporting medical evidence and increasingly stronger legislation, the National Transportation Safety Board reports that driving while impaired is the most frequently committed crime in the United States.[11] Approximately 1.5 million drivers were arrested in 2000 alone for driving under the influence—and these were only the ones who were caught. For every DUI driver arrested, an estimated 200 to 2,000 DUI drivers go undetected.[12]

Alcohol slows the brain's ability to process data and make decisions. The more alcohol consumed, the more impaired the decision-making process becomes. Therefore, someone who consumes a large amount of alcohol will become significantly impaired. As consumption continues, progressively slower and more erroneous decisions about controlling a vehicle will be made.

I believe that a good number of today's teenage drivers do not intentionally set out to get drunk before driving. In my opinion, most want to try and make good decisions about driving. However, when drivers do drink and/or take drugs, they are forced into having to make a go or no-go (drive/don't drive) decision. Young drivers lack the education, experience, and foresight to look at the big picture and understand the magnitude of deciding to get behind the wheel and drive while impaired. They do not think two steps ahead and do not anticipate pending issues. More experienced drivers don't have those excuses. Adult drivers who drive while impaired are not inexperienced; they are just irresponsible.

For the multiple repeat DUI offender who continues to drive time and time again while impaired, forget about it: Identifying and understanding the previously discussed five traps will be of no value to them. However, for the young driver who is inexperienced and one night finds himself wrestling with the decision to drive or not drive, knowing of these five traps may help him think harder and make a safer decision. Knowing that they control decisions made for both their personal and opportunistic zones of the POP zone defense should cause any younger driver to think hard. Having to even contemplate driving or not driving should automatically invoke the err-to-conservative rule. The conservative and safer decision is to not drive.

Being the Passenger of an Impaired Driver

Surveys have shown that far too many youths believe they have ridden as a passenger in a vehicle operated by a peer who should not have been at the controls due to impairment. The National Institute on Drug Abuse reported that 25 percent of vehicle passengers age 16–20 reported riding in a car with a driver they felt had consumed too much alcohol.[13] I believe it takes more courage and responsibility for teens to avoid riding as passengers of impaired drivers than it does for teens to keep themselves from driving impaired. Peer pressure and peer evaluations play a major role in young adults succumbing to the pressure to ride as a passenger of a friend who is driving while impaired.

A teen may not be able to prevent the person they rode to an event with from drinking and driving, but they can prevent themselves from leaving the event with that same person. Like their personal defense zone, they also have control or influence over their immediate surroundings within their opportunistic zone.

Making a commitment to not drive while impaired and committing to not riding with an impaired driver is a good pledge for teenagers to make, both to themselves and to their parents. Their decision to avoid a scenario like this allows them to immediately take control of and secure both their personal POP defense zone as well as their immediate surroundings or their opportunistic POP zone. However, many stop there, not realizing the significance of leaving the entire participative defensive zone unmanaged.

The opportunistic zone creates an opportunity for a teen to influence her surroundings. She has the choice not to get in a car with an impaired driver and thus has the opportunity to exert influence on her own safety. As in her personal zone, she has decision-making responsibilities and privileges. She is in control of making decisions that influence her own surroundings.

Recognizing Impaired Drivers

So your young driver has pledged not to drink and drive and has also pledged not to ride with a driver under the influence. Is he safe from alcohol or drug-related impairment accidents? No way.

As stated earlier, a high percentage of impaired drivers are not caught and thus remain on the roads. In addition, studies show that over half of the drivers jailed for DUI offenses are repeat offenders.[14] These statistics indicate that all drivers, including younger drivers just starting out, need to proactively watch for potentially reckless DUI drivers who share the road.

As we have already discussed, drivers do not have direct control over their participative POP zone. Similarly, pilots do not have control over much of the environment around them. They cannot control the weather, aircraft component failure, and aircraft under the control of other pilots. Because of this lack of direct control, pilots have learned to be extremely proactive in managing their participative zone by looking for the first signs of trouble and then reacting to them in a defensive manner.

A good pilot will be diligent in looking out for and managing any threat that occurs during her flight. Similarly, drivers face threats from their participative zone. This is why the previously mentioned Pilot-Driver concepts of anticipate, see and avoid, proactively look for trouble, expect the unexpected, and build your outs are so important to flying. These concepts are tools that allow for the better management and early recognition of threats within the participative POP zone.

Drivers who anticipate encountering an impaired driver and drivers who are proactively looking for signs of other drivers under the influence are starting to manage the threat that coexists alongside them. The participative POP zone is a highly reactive zone so the sooner trouble is detected, the sooner an evasive reaction can be executed. Therefore, being reactionary, a sober driver needs to see and avoid impaired drivers.

The U.S. Department of Transportation completed a study in 2001 to try and find ways of detecting drunk or impaired drivers. Their results indicate that there are some telling cues that can alert a driver or passenger if a nearby driver is driving under the influence. Their study shows that witnessing any one of these cues during daylight hours yields a 25 percent to 90 percent chance that the driver exhibiting these behaviors is impaired. In addition, the probability that a driver is impaired increases if any one of these cues is seen during nighttime. The rate of alcohol involvement in fatal crashes is more than three times as high at night as during the day (63 percent versus 19 percent).[15] When two or more cues are witnessed, the probability greatly increases. These cues are broken down into four categories:

1. *Problems in maintaining proper lane position*

- Weaving within lane lines
- Weaving across lane lines
- Straddling a lane line
- Drifting
- Swerving
- Almost striking or actually hitting a parked vehicle or other object
- Making a turn with a wider radius than is required
- Drifting during a turn (often crosses a lane line while turning)

2. *Speed and braking problems*

- Stopping problems (stopping too far from a curb, too far from a stop light, too far from a stop sign or stopping at an improper angle to a curb)
- Accelerating for no reason
- Varying speed
- Traveling at a slower than posted speed (usually 10 MPH slower or more)

3. *Vigilance*

- Driving without headlights at night
- Failure to signal
- Inconsistent signal (left turn signal is on but driver executes a right turn)
- Driving in opposing lanes
- Driving the wrong way on a one-way street
- Slow response to traffic signals
- Stopped in a road lane for no apparent reason

4. Judgment problems

- Following too closely to another vehicle
- Improper or unsafe lane change
- Improper turn
- Driving on other than a designated roadway
- Inappropriate or unusual behavior

In addition, a driver appearing to be physically drinking from a container or acting impatient and rude are also signs of impaired drivers. These cues were documented from studying over 5,000 traffic stops and two field research sessions.

These cues are to help the driver proactively manage their environment. These cues, in conjunction with the PilotDriver concepts, are tools that allow a driver to better see and avoid and thus better manager their participation POP zone.

Motorcycle DUI Recognition Cues

In a separate study on motorcycle DUI detection cues, excellent and good cue categories were developed. Many cues overlap with those related to the operation of automobiles and trucks but a few are obviously solely related to the operation of a motorcycle.

Excellent Cues (50 percent or greater probability that the driver is DUI)

- Drifting during a turn or curve.
- Having trouble with balance at a stop.
- Having trouble with a dismount.
- Having problems with turning (unsteady, improper lean angle; sudden corrections).
- Weaving.
- Exhibiting inappropriate behavior such as carrying objects. When a motorcycle driver has one arm around a case of beer and the other is on the handlebar, that would be an inappropriate behavior.

Good Cues (30 to 50 percent probability that the driver is DUI)

- Exhibiting erratic movements while going straight.
- Operating without lights at night.
- Operating recklessly.
- Tailgating.

- Running a stop light or stop sign.
- Traveling the wrong way on a one-way street.

Seeing and Avoiding Impaired Drivers

All drivers should commit to themselves to be proactively vigilant in profiling other drivers and vehicles to find and avoid those who appear to pose a threat. Like an FBI profiler, look at characteristics and try to prioritize what surrounding vehicles might pose the greatest threat.

Some drivers have serious drinking and drug problems and they are a threat to all drivers, pedestrians, and bystanders. I recently read a story about a little girl who was run over and killed by someone driving under the influence—while playing in her own driveway. It was even more upsetting when it was reported that this was the driver's sixteenth DUI offense; he was driving with a suspended license and no insurance. These are the people you need to profile and attempt to pick out using the cues just listed. See and avoid, proactively look for trouble, and expect the unexpected. These are the people you need to help your young driver learn how to recognize and avoid.

Have you had this discussion with your young driver? The discussion about how one single careless action can change his or her life, your life, and the lives of many others forever? It is a discussion worth having. Get your young driver to describe the worst-case scenario that he or she alone could create by driving impaired. Your input will further amplify the example and the resulting scenario will usually help the young driver to think about the consequences. Also discuss how the five traps discussed previously might lure a young driver into driving while impaired—that not only does your young driver have to be responsible, but that he or she also has to look out for and be responsible for seeing and avoiding the irresponsible drivers.

Remember that many impaired drivers end up driving simply because they feel they have no other means to get to their final destination. Give your teen a "golden pass" to call you at any time under any conditions for a lift home. By evoking this pass, you agree you will safely get her home and she will not be asked any questions (at least not until the following day). Teens will eventually find themselves at the wrong end of a bad decision. It is natural and part of growing up and if a child knows she has this pass, it might help prevent driving under the influence, an accident, or worse.

Review

- It is prohibited in all 50 states for a driver under the age of 21 to consume any amount of alcohol or illegal drugs. Period.
- The level and effects of BAC increase exponentially with each drink. Some level of impairment begins with the first drink.
- While under the influence of drugs and/or alcohol, reaction time degradation is exponential, not linear.
- The likelihood of being involved in an accident while under the influence of drugs and/or alcohol is exponential, not linear.
- After drinking, young drivers often elect to drive because they feel they do not have any alternatives. Parents should repeatedly encourage their teens to call if they find themselves drinking or stuck riding with a drunk driver.
- It has been documented that alcohol consumption increases other risky behavior.
- The five younger-driver DUI traps are synergistic and often combine to exponentially increase the likelihood of an accident.
- Teenagers should use the personal and opportunistic zones to directly reduce their chances of an accident.
- Teenage drivers should use the visual detection cues of recognizing DUI drivers as part of their participative POP zone defense to avoid being hit by other drivers. The effects of alcohol and/or drugs are inconsistent in a given individual because of several changing factors like diet, sleep, and other medication. Teenagers often build a competency silo that falsely leads them to believe that because, for example, they had five beers last Friday the effect will be the same this Friday and they will be competent to drive after having five beers.
- Pilot habits that apply to avoiding impaired drivers are anticipation, building your outs, erring to the conservative, avoiding compounding events, proactively look for trouble, having situational awareness, thinking two steps ahead, seeing and avoiding, breaking the trend, and avoiding get-there-itis.

Chapter 10
Pedestrian Avoidance

Each year, approximately 6,000 pedestrians are killed and another 100,000 are injured as a result of traffic accidents.[1] Nearly one in every five traffic fatalities involves a pedestrian.

Drivers not paying attention and proactively looking for pedestrians, especially where they are not expected to be, can find themselves involved in a pedestrian/vehicle accident. Data collected in 2000 and 2001 indicate four high probability environments for pedestrian/vehicle fatalities.[2] They are:

1. Urban areas (69 percent)
2. Non-intersection locations (79 percent)
3. Normal weather conditions (90 percent)
4. Night (64 percent)

In addition, there are four other environments that offer a high potential for pedestrian/vehicle crashes. It behooves the aware driver to pay extra attention to the following environments:

1. Railroad crossings. Pedestrians have difficulty judging the distance and speed a train is traveling—especially at night
2. Construction work zones where there are several distractions for drivers, pedestrians, and workers
3. High-speed roadways where drivers usually do not expect to encounter pedestrians
4. Areas where sidewalks are not provided

Walk Alert

To promote pedestrian safety and to educate drivers on risks associated with pedestrian cohabitation, the National Highway Traffic Safety Administration, the American Automobile Association, and the National Safety Council, along with several local community groups created a national safety program called Walk Alert for pedestrians. The overall goal is to reduce pedestrian accidents and fatalities.

Although anyone can be involved in pedestrian accidents, Walk Alert data documents three groups of pedestrians who are more likely than others to be involved in an accident. Drivers should therefore be particularly vigilant in recognizing and monitoring the movement of these three pedestrian groups. The three groups are:

1. Children
2. Elderly adults
3. Pedestrians whose judgment is impaired by drugs or alcohol

A driver needs to be on the lookout for pedestrians of any age. Knowing some of the behaviors that often put pedestrians in harms way of being hit by a vehicle will better prepare a driver for anticipating and avoiding a potential accident. Young drivers should be on the lookout for the following common pedestrian behaviors.

Children

Approximately 22 percent of all children 5 to 9 years of age who were killed in traffic accidents were pedestrians.[3] Children are not fully aware of safety issues. They are impulsive and often have difficulty paying constant attention to accident prevention. Drivers need to use extra caution when around younger children or when around parked cars where younger children congregate such as schools, residential areas, and parking lots. Anticipate that every child you see is going to run in front of your vehicle. Also assume that every child in a parking lot, whether in clear view or not, does not see you.

Overall, children as a group have difficulty in:

- Judging whether a car is moving or stopped.
- Judging the boundaries of a road.
- Seeing objects and movement outside their field of vision, which is smaller than an adult's field of vision.

Preschoolers

Common behaviors jeopardizing preschoolers are:

- **Darting out.** Children are often preoccupied with their play activities and dart out into the road or surrounding driveways while playing games or chasing a ball. Most of these types of accidents happen within a block of the victim's home.

- **Crossing behind a vehicle that is backing up.** Preschoolers are tiny and often crawl and hide, making it difficult for drivers to see them. Simply checking a rearview mirror prior to backing up is not good enough to clear the area. Family vans, trucks, and sport utility vehicles can easily conceal a small child from the driver's vision.
- **Playing in a driveway or roadway.** Preschoolers may be struck while playing in a roadway or riding a tricycle, skateboard, or wagon into a roadway.

Children Kindergarten Through Grade 3

Common types of behaviors jeopardizing children of this age group include:

- Darting into a driveway or roadway.
- Going to and from an ice cream truck.
- Crossing in front of a stopped bus.
- Running across an intersection.
- Playing in a driveway or roadway.

Children in Grades 4 Through 6

Common types of behaviors jeopardizing children in grades 4 through 6 include:

- Darting into a roadway or driveway.
- Crossing in front of a turning vehicle.
- Running across an intersection.
- Crossing a multilane street.
- Entering or crossing an intersection.
- Playing in a driveway or roadway.
- Going to or from a school bus.
- Crossing behind a vehicle that is backing up.
- Walking between cars in a parking lot.

Junior High School Students

Common types of behaviors jeopardizing junior high or middle school students include:

- Crossing multilane roadways.
- Navigating complex intersections.

- Walking at night without proper attire or illumination to warn oncoming drivers of their presence.

High School Students

Common types of behaviors jeopardizing high school students include:

- Alcohol and/or drug impaired decision making.
- Jaywalking outside of an official crosswalk with pedestrian traffic control.
- Walking at night without proper attire or illumination to warn oncoming drivers of their presence.

Adults

Collisions between pedestrians and vehicles at intersections present the greatest problem for adults who are walking. Pedestrians hit while walking in the roadway represent about 20 percent of crashes involving adults age 25 through 64 and approximately 30 percent of the crashes for adults age 20 through 24. Between 35 and 45 percent of all adult pedestrian/vehicle crashes involve alcohol. The BAC of fatally injured adult pedestrians averages twice the level found in adults involved in other traffic fatalities. The irony of this statistic is that some people who realize they have had too much to drink elect to walk rather than drive but may still end up in a pedestrian accident due to walking under the influence.[4]

Alcohol involvement for either the driver or pedestrian was reported in 47 percent of the traffic crashes that resulted in a pedestrian fatality.[5]

Children present a safety threat to drivers because of their lack of focus on playing safe or acting in a responsible or safe manner. They simply want to play and tend to be less vigilant in trying to avoid an accident. Adults for the most part take an active role in participating in accident avoidance. They know to look for traffic before crossing a street. There are, however, three behaviors that increase the chances of an adult being hit by a vehicle:

- Walking in the roadway.
- Alcohol and/or drug impaired decision making.
- Walking at night without proper illumination to warn oncoming drivers of their presence.

Okay, let's process this data for a moment. The most common situations surrounding adult pedestrian accidents are walking in the roadway, being impaired with alcohol, and being hard to see at night. Hmm—and these are the adults! These top three reasons for adult pedestrian accidents scream irresponsibility.

This is a good time to highlight that the PilotDriver concepts and pilot habits can be used in situations other than driving a vehicle. For example, a pedestrian walking at night and wearing dark clothes might want to anticipate that other drivers may not see him. 25 percent of drivers striking a pedestrian in the dark report that they never saw the pedestrian prior to impact.[6] Automobile headlights are usually set to shine a bit right of center and this makes it more difficult to illuminate and detect cars and pedestrians approaching from the left.

Thinking two steps ahead might lead to wearing appropriate clothing to improve visibility and possibly carrying a light.

Elderly Adults

Young drivers can anticipate that elderly pedestrians can increase the odds of being hit with the following three behaviors:

- Crossing at intersections.
- Crossing behind a vehicle that is backing up.
- Being difficult for drivers to see.

Strategies for Drivers

Expecting the unexpected and predicting situations will help drivers prepare to better manage pedestrians. Drivers should examine their environments in an attempt to anticipate likely situations. For example, while driving through a residential neighborhood, drivers might anticipate children darting out in the road, especially from between parked cars and from behind objects such as bushes, trash cans, mailboxes, and the like. Drivers in this environment should be anticipating children running in front of them, playing in the streets, and perhaps walking behind a vehicle that is backing up. A ball or toy moving into the street is a sure sign that a small child is likely to follow close behind.

While driving through a busy urban area with adult pedestrian traffic, watch out for jaywalkers. Studies indicate that alcohol-related decision impairment plays a large role in pedestrian accidents, so be prepared for pedestrians making poor and unexpected decisions. Driving through a college town on a weekend or early in the morning should put both drivers and pedestrians on guard. Drunk pedestrians and drunk drivers are a bad combination.

Being aware of one's environment provides drivers the opportunity to quickly examine their surrounding participation zone. This allows for a mental rundown of scenarios that are most likely to occur. Anticipating the probabilities based on the circumstances leads to higher driver awareness and a quicker reaction time because the driver is already somewhat prepared to encounter a particular circumstance.

Pedestrian Safety Strategies

When not driving, many of us become pedestrians. In keeping with one of my previously stated goals of reducing the odds of your young driver being in an accident, I want to have a quick discussion about what can be done, as a pedestrian, to also reduce the odds of being involved in a vehicle collision.

As a pedestrian, it is imperative to be aware of how drivers are going to try and spoil your day. Separation from the flow of traffic is important. For example, if given the choice of walking on or directly beside a road versus walking next to that same road behind a wall or barrier, choose to use the wall or barrier as further separation from the road. It is an extra precaution in separating you, the pedestrian, from traffic.

Having repeatedly heard about a driver's need to anticipate their surrounding events, pedestrians should also anticipate that drivers do not see them. Even while crossing inside a designated crosswalk area with the illuminated "Walk" indication, the path may not be clear. Once a "Walk" sign illuminates indicating it should be safe for pedestrians to cross, look each direction and then look one last time in the direction from which the traffic should be coming. Remember that as a car turns a corner, the front support section of the roof will at some point pass through the driver's field of view. Ideally, eye contact with the driver should be made and kept while crossing.

PilotDrivers are always looking for the unexpected, so as a pedestrian, anticipate that something out of the ordinary will threaten your safety. "Normal" and courteous drivers will typically not be a threat to pedestrians, but they can be. Distractions, mechanical failures, and so forth could cause a pedestrian accident with any driver. However, looking for the unexpected is a good focus. Expect the unexpected. A motorcycle driving on the sidewalk or a drunk driver not paying attention present a threat to pedestrians.

Bicyclists

More than one-fifth of the bicyclists killed in traffic crashes in 2001 were between 5 and 15 years old. Alcohol was reported in more than one-third of the bicyclist fatalities in 2001.[7]

Pedestrians typically tend to congregate at crosswalks. Bicyclists can be at any intersection or riding with traffic along the roadway. At first, young drivers have a tendency to fully concentrate on their vehicle and the other vehicles around them. Concentration on looking for pedestrians and bicyclists may be lacking. Bicyclists will usually fall into a driver's blind spot, especially when either the driver or bicyclist is making a turn.

Review

- Crosswalks around bars and public events may contain pedestrians who have consumed alcohol and are less careful.
- By combining the type of surrounding environment (housing development or a college bar area), along with the age of the pedestrian (child, teen, or adult), drivers can profile the situation and be on the lookout for certain potential threats conducive to that combination.
- Try to make eye contact or observe where a pedestrian's eyes are looking in an attempt to anticipate their actions.
- Pilot habits that apply to pedestrian awareness are anticipation, expecting the unexpected, proactively looking for trouble, having situational awareness, and seeing and avoiding.

Chapter 11
Drowsy Driving

In a 1996 report, data from the National Highway Traffic Safety Administration (NHTSA) indicated that police reports showed that roughly 56,000 vehicle crashes annually are directly tied to drowsiness, fatigue, and inattention. Drowsiness means dull response characterized by sleepiness and fatigue means physical or mental weariness resulting from exertion. Driver inattention refers to "day dreaming," preoccupation and distractions that take the driver's focus away from concentrating on safe vehicle operation. They document 40,000 nonfatal injuries and 1,550 fatalities resulting from these crashes.[1]

Many experts in the driving safety field believe these statistics underreport the actual number of accidents caused by drowsy driving. Not all drivers survive an accident to report feeling drowsy and many accident reports cite the result like "failure to maintain lane control" instead of the cause "fell asleep at the wheel." Researchers estimate that lack of sleep contributes to anywhere from 1 to 10 percent of the 20 million automobile accidents that occur each year in the United States.[2]

Drivers at Greatest Risk

Any driver is susceptible to an accident when they drive while drowsy, but the National Highway Traffic Safety Administration reports that three groups of people are at higher-than-average risk for accidents attributable to drowsy driving or actually falling asleep at the wheel.[3] They are:

1. Young people, in this case under the age of 30, account for almost two-thirds of drowsy driving crashes. This is a large number considering this age group only represents about one-fourth of licensed drivers. These younger drivers were four times more likely to have a crash related to drowsy driving than those drivers over 30 years old.

In addition to learning how to drive, testing their boundaries, and experimenting with risks, this age group is also susceptible to changes in physical maturity (requiring more sleep), changes in sleep patterns (irregular work hours, all night studying), and cultural and lifestyle changes (late night parties and entertainment). In particular, males from the under 30 age group were more likely to drive while drowsy than were females of the same age.

2. Shift workers whose sleep is irregular due to inconsistent work hours. Night-shift workers typically get 1.5 fewer hours of sleep per 24 hours than day-shift workers. The circadian sleep cycle or internal "24-hour clock" is usually disrupted for shift workers, especially those working the midnight to early morning shift. In one study, close to 95 percent of night nurses working 12-hour shifts reported having had an automobile accident or near-miss accident while driving home from work.

3. Individuals with sleep disorders like sleep apnea and narcolepsy. Sleep apnea is a condition in which breathing patterns are interrupted during sleep, which cause the patient to get less-than-desirable amounts of oxygen. It leads to exhaustion and feeling run down despite the fact that the patient reports having slept most of the night. It has been estimated that approximately 18 million Americans have sleep apnea. Narcolepsy is a condition characterized by sudden and uncontrollable attacks of deep sleep and is a potentially disabling condition. Its primary symptom is a feeling of tiredness during the daytime.

The NHTSA recognized that drowsy-driving accidents are a growing problem. Crash investigations now seek drowsy-driving attributes as a possible cause of an accident causing these statistics to rise. They initiated a major effort with Congressional backing to establish an education program on the effects of fatigue on driving. Together with the National Center on Sleep Disorders Research, the NHTSA established a program with three main arms:

1. A school-based program for high school students to increase their awareness about the dangers of driving while drowsy.
2. A work-based program helping companies educate their employees who work shifts with irregular hours.
3. An in-vehicle data-collection initiative to better collect and analyze driver and vehicle performance in real-life events.

The first two are self-explanatory and relate to the two groups of drivers with the highest likelihood of becoming drowsy while driving. The last point about in-vehicle data collection, however, is interesting. Experts agree that statistics relating to drowsy driving are hard to collect and analyze because drivers do not always realize that an accident or near-accident was caused by the effects of driving drowsy. One does not have to physically fall asleep to have a drowsy-driving accident. A driver in the early stages of drowsiness might not fall asleep at the wheel but could very well have her reaction time impaired by fatigue or by not paying attention.

The American Automobile Association (AAA) Foundation for Traffic Safety funded a study to answer the question "How accurately can people judge the chance that they will fall asleep in the next two minutes on a scale from 0 to 100 percent?" In order to make the exercise relevant to a sleepy driver, two minutes was selected as the time threshold because it was short enough for the subjects to reasonably understand its duration but long enough to allow the subjects time to take some form of corrective action. A group of 42 healthy male and female subjects between the ages of 17 and 22 participated in the study.

The study established that people do, in fact, have a limited ability to accurately predict the onset of sleep while driving.[4] Since drivers in general do a poor job of predicting the onset of sleep, there is a high potential for falling asleep while behind the wheel and causing a severe accident.

Completely falling asleep behind the wheel is only part of the problem, though. Merely feeling drowsy while driving can significantly increase the likelihood of causing accidents. Drivers who continue to drive a vehicle while feeling drowsy will usually experience a diminished awareness of their surroundings (decreased situational awareness). In addition, they tend to require more time to process data and make decisions, leading to a slower reaction time (increased decision compression). A citation for an accident may state "failure to control the vehicle" when in actuality the catalyst for the accident was driving while drowsy.

According to many experts, teenagers who drive while tired, let alone those who actually fall asleep behind the wheel, present a real safety problem. Most teenagers require nine hours of sleep per night, yet on average only receive six point five hours per night.[5]

Individuals who gradually lose one to two hours of sleep at night can create "sleep debt." Over time, this can lead to chronic sleepiness because sleep debt is cumulative. These drivers who gradually lose sleep over time are at equal or even greater risk than the driver who pulled an "all-nighter" by staying up the previous night. Both types of drivers can easily reduce their driving performance level while feeling drowsy and could even fall asleep behind the wheel.

The Circadian Sleep Cycle

Homeostatic and circadian factors both govern the sleep-wake cycle. Homeostasis relates to the neurobiological requirement for sleep; the longer the period of wakefulness, the greater the need for sleep and the more difficult it is to resist. The circadian pacemaker, or "internal clock" if you will, completes one cycle approximately every 24 to 25 hours. The word *circadian* is Latin and comes from *circa diem* meaning about a day. Homeostatic variables influence circadian factors to regulate the timing of sleepiness and wakefulness.

These processes create a fairly predictable pattern of two sleepiness peaks. For people who normally sleep during the night, one sleepiness peak commonly occurs during the afternoon and one at night.[6] The sleep-wake cycle is also influenced by the light-dark cycle, which for most people means being awake while it's light out and asleep while it's dark. When individuals are not synchronized with this pattern, they can experience sleep loss and sleep disruption, which in turn can reduce alertness. Night-shift workers, travelers crossing time zones, and air crews are examples of people who are out of phase with the normal sleep-wake cycle. This explains why shift workers who work at night or who work irregular hours are at higher risk of engaging in drowsy driving.

An interesting graph can be plotted by using the time of day when police-reported accidents were attributed to a sleepy driver. Segregating the drivers who caused the accidents into four age groups, the plot suggests that drivers under 26 years of age tend to have two peak times of accidents related to drowsiness. The first accident peak is in the early morning hours. This makes sense for the average person who has night-time sleeping habits and who has stayed up into the early morning hours. Late afternoon hours were also a peak accident time for this age group. Parents should keep these two peak accident times in mind when educating their teenage drivers on risks to be aware of and how to prevent accidents.

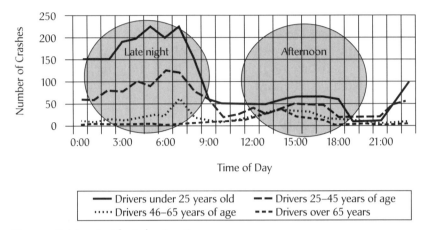

Drowsy Driving Accidents by Age Group
National Highway Traffic Safety Administration. *Drowsy Driving and Automobile Crashes: Report and Recommendations.* Washington, D.C.: National Highway Traffic Safety Administration, 1998: 9–10.

Remember that research has shown that most people cannot accurately predict whether they will fall asleep within two minutes. It then becomes especially troubling to consider the profiles of two "typical" teenagers. The first profile is of a young driver who regularly gets less than the recommended nine hours of sleep per night. He is losing sleep over a period of time and may be accumulating sleep debt which in turn increases his odds of driving while drowsy. I don't know many high school students getting nine hours of sleep per night. The second profile is that of a teenager working irregular shifts, especially after school and on weekends. Not having a regular sleeping pattern puts a driver at risk for drowsy driving.

Countermeasures for Drowsiness

There are several countermeasures that can be used to combat the effects of drowsiness while driving. Consuming caffeine has been studied with varying conclusions. Although it can be argued that taking caffeine can improve alertness, it is by no means a substitute for sleep. Caffeine from coffee, soda, tea, or candy can take 30 or more minutes to enter the bloodstream. A driver who is very sleepy and drinks coffee can still have microsleeps, which are tiny naps lasting perhaps just a few seconds, but long enough to drift out of a road lane and cause an accident.[7] In addition, although caffeine may help keep drivers from falling asleep, they can still suffer from reduced reaction and decision time from being tired.

Another countermeasure that can be used to combat drowsy driving is switching drivers. If switching drivers is not an option, a good alternative is to pull off the road and take a nap. Studies have shown that even a brief 15 to 20 minute nap can improve subsequent performance. Be aware that drivers who nap in excess of 20 minutes are usually groggy after they awake, so take some time to get re-acclimated prior to driving. Young drivers who start to feel drowsy while driving should realize that a probable series of compounding events is starting to take place. A proper course of action is to break the trend of unfolding events and take a break.

Of course, medication, alcohol, and a driver's attitude can serve to vary the onset of drowsiness. Once again, exponentiation and compounding problems will most likely combine to make matters worse.

Review

- Driving while drowsy is believed to be a bigger problem than studies portray because of the difficulty in obtaining accurate crash data.
- Police reports have documented that young drivers are more often involved in crashes resulting from falling asleep while driving. These often occur during the early morning and late afternoon hours.
- Young drivers are susceptible to driving while drowsy.
- Drowsiness levels vary and hinder response and reaction time as well as judgment. A driver does not have to fall asleep to realize the negative effects of drowsiness.
- Studies show that people do a poor job of predicting when they are about to fall asleep.
- Pilot habits that apply drowsy driving are anticipation, considering compounding events, thinking two steps ahead, breaking the trend, and avoiding get-there-itis.

Chapter 12
Distractions

Driver distraction is a major contributor to crashes. The NHTSA estimates that approximately 25 percent of police-documented crashes involve driver inattention.

Inattention is caused by any event or circumstance that consumes even a tiny fraction of a driver's dedication to safely operating his or her vehicle. Driver inattention results in a reduction in concentration and focus. Several forms of inattention can intermix or happen during a driving trip.

The most common forms of inattention affecting drivers are also the same forms that pilots deal with and sometimes struggle to recognize and manage:

1. **Distraction.** A diversion in focus resulting from a force or event happening simultaneously when driving.
2. **Preoccupation.** A diversion in focus resulting from thinking about an event or situation that is not happening simultaneously when driving.
3. **Absorption.** Being fixated and absorbed with a particular task while neglecting to perform other important safety tasks.

Distractions: Simple and Complex

Flying in and of itself is challenging and this challenge is compounded by things constantly changing. Original flight plans and routes of flight and sometimes even destinations are continually changed and updated. Air traffic control may assign a route that varies from the originally planned route, which is a distraction. Turbulent weather is a distraction. Navigation equipment problems, engine problems, and the surrounding air traffic are all distractions. In fact, I can say with confidence that distractions are a common part of flying and a good pilot needs to be able to deal with them while remaining focused on keeping the aircraft and passengers safe.

Distractions are so common in flying and such a standard variable of every flight, that flight instructors teach distraction recognition and management skills to students. Flight examiners will purposely create distractions for pilots taking FAA flight tests to ensure the applicant can divide his attention between managing a distraction, or multiple distractions, while remaining in control of the aircraft and its flight. It is mandatory that pilots learn to divide their attention and manage distractions.

With approximately 80 percent of general aviation aircraft accidents attributed to pilot error and 80 percent of automobile accidents attributed to driver error, the recognition and management of inattention and distractions is important, especially for young drivers who are just learning to drive. Distractions for pilots and drivers are often part of the early foundation of compounding events that can quickly spiral into a critical situation. Distractions can be broken down into two groups: simple and complex.

Simple distractions take place in the background and often a driver can deal with them without diverting from the original focus of safely operating the vehicle. Drivers usually do not even register encountering a simple distraction because they coexist within the driver's environment. However, several simple distractions can compound together to cause attention diversion. Complex distractions force drivers to change their vision and look in a different direction. They force drivers to look somewhere else other than the road or traffic flow in front of their moving vehicle and/or to think about a situation and consider one or multiple reactions.

This table illustrates a few of the many types of distractions drivers encounter. Often several can happen together, making a situation more complicated than it may originally appear.

Table 12.1   Driver Distractions

Simple Distractions	Complex Distractions
Listening to music	Turning to talk with passengers while dialing a cell phone
Casual conversation with a passenger	Driving in heavy rain while looking for a CD case under the seat
Flipping down a sun visor	Having an impatient driver following you in severe sun glare
Activating a turn indicator	Crying children in the back seat with a passing ambulance in a busy intersection
Opening a window	Rowdy passengers throwing objects inside the car

Remember our earlier example showing that it takes an average of 38 car lengths to stop the average car in normal conditions at 55 miles per hour? Distractions and their negative impact on delaying recognition and reaction times can often be the variable that makes or breaks the ability to stop in time in order to avoid having an accident.

Think of the human brain as a single-event sequential processor. By nature, it usually focuses its processing power on the current task and then, when that task is complete, it refocuses the majority of its processing power on the next task, and so on. It is difficult for the human brain to simultaneously undertake multiple tasks. With time and some experience, operating a vehicle for a young driver will become second nature and for the most part, it becomes routine. Drivers move down the road without constantly thinking about every driving detail or decision. The driving process flows and the human brain is happy thinking about one event at a time and then moving to the next event that needs to be thought about.

However, when multiple distractions occur in rapid succession or even simultaneously, drivers may think they are trying to solve all situations at once but in reality, they are focusing on each individual problem, one at a time. Each individual issue may receive just a fraction of a second's brain power, but each event is still being processed singularly.

For example, say a driver is in heavy traffic with young children fighting in the backseat—and say the disk in the CD player is skipping—and say a bee is flying around the inside of the car, causing the fighting kids to totally freak out. This is a complex distraction scenario because multiple events are happening and the driver is most likely looking away from the road to see what all the commotion is about inside the car. Part of the driver's focus is now diverted from total concentration on driving the car. Attention and processing power are divided between driving the car, fixing a CD, surveying the surrounding traffic, refereeing the fighting kids, and avoiding a bee. The driver may start to worry about the bee, but then realize the congested traffic poses a more serious threat so they refocus on the surrounding traffic. Then, after processing the traffic status, the driver flips to the next issue and eliminates the CD problem by turning it off. But focus on driving was lost again for a moment to fix the CD problem. Now the driver refocuses on the bee and realizes that the screaming kids will most likely not calm down until the bee issue is resolved.

It is easy to get caught up in solving multiple problems inside the car and to lose focus on controlling the moving car. Trying to solve multiple problems takes time and in many scenarios causes confusion because the resolution for one issue most likely has an impact on solving the remaining issues. Confusion elongates processing time and, in many cases, causes the driver to second guess his original solution. Confusion and second guessing delay a resolution, chewing up valuable stopping distance and opportunities to break the trend.

Those distractions discussed previously are examples of distractions that are in a driver's control because the driver can elect to pull over, terminate the bee, and settle the kids down. These distractions fall within the opportunistic POP zone because they are in the driver's immediate surroundings with the opportunity to influence or change them.

Suppose on top of this bee scenario, an impatient driver is tailgating our distracted driver and contemplating a dangerous pass. In addition, the distracted driver has now entered a thunderstorm with heavy rain. These events further compound the situation as the complex distractions increase. Think about the power of all these distractions combining to exponentially increase the odds of having an accident. All this is happening while the car is moving at some rate of speed along the roadway.

Rain and a tailgating driver are not in the direct control of the driver and the driver cannot influence their behavior, so these two new distractions fall into the participative POP zone. How does a driver manage such a situation? The distracted driver has the opportunity to influence and change the screaming kids and the bee but must coexist with the other driver and the weather. The best defense for the distracted driver in the participative zone is to see and avoid. Clearly the first step is even being able to recognize the trend of building and compounding events. I would advise the distracted driver to pull over and let the tailgating driver pass, and while waiting for the rain to subside, whack the bee and flip the kiddies some Cheerios.

Trying to manage all of these compounding events while safely controlling a moving car would put a lot of demands on our single stage processor brain. The problem for humans is that these problem and distraction variables are not always sequential but often simultaneous. All of these variables interact together and it is difficult to make fast and accurate driving decisions. Losing even three-quarters of a second of perception time or processing time or reaction time can easily burn up over 60 feet of roadway.

Again, our concept of compounding events becomes relevant. Many drivers can manage to safely operate a vehicle while successfully dealing with a few simple distractions at any one point in time. Sometimes even managing a few simple distractions combined with some complex distractions is possible. Managing any combination of distractions seems to get easier with driving experience. However, it does not take long for young drivers to successfully manage a few distractions and then proclaim themselves experienced and competent in overall distraction management. They falsely build a competency silo, believing that they are able to handle any and all combinations of distractions because they successfully managed some last week.

This trap of falsely building competency silos warrants concern, because even a few distractions coexisting with compounding events and decision compression create a difficult scenario that requires taking time to detect the problems, process them, and then make the correct decision. The more issues requiring decisions, the more likely confusion and second guessing will come into play, thus causing further delays. This all ties back to task saturation and the whopping 80 percent error in driver decision making. Remember that the majority of general aviation accidents attributed to pilot error happen at times that are most prone to decision compression and task saturation like takeoffs and landings.

Distractions can really cause trouble when one has to process them while controlling the vehicle and making decisions in a short amount of time—like seconds or milliseconds. Approaching an intersection with all the previously mentioned distractions and then having to make a split-second decision on how to best yield to an emergency vehicle while simultaneously avoiding a driver who just ran a red light forces drivers to do what the brain is really poor at doing—and that is simultaneously processing multiple events and their associated interdependencies. Compound this further with a brand-new driver who perhaps has not yet encountered an impatient driver or an emergency vehicle or a storm with a heavy rain and events and their associated decision pressures start to shoot out of control.

Inexperienced driving combined with inexperience in handling distractions and making rapid multiple decisions often forces drivers, especially younger drivers, into a panic. It can be visual as they physically show signs of panic such as facial expressions, body language, and nervousness, or it can be a thinking panic where the brain does not do a good job of managing multiple decisions and keeps alternating between possible decisions without deciding on any solutions. Even if a younger driver happens to muster a half-decent response to a unfamiliar critical situation, he or she often tends to immediately second guess their initial reaction due to a lack of previous experience with that particular scenario. This fuels decision compression.

Sixteen-year-old drivers lead the field for fatal crashes involving driver error (80 percent), speeding (36 percent), and vehicles with more than three occupants (33 percent). This is statistical confirmation that the inexperienced driver does not do well in managing distractions, compounding events, and critical decisions in an extremely short time while under task saturation.

It does not matter if young drivers are honor students or star athletes, they are all relatively inexperienced at driving and being forced to make critical decisions under pressure with out-of-their-control variables makes them extremely vulnerable to accidents. They quickly build a competency silo labeled "I can drive safely" because they have done it previously under "normal" driving conditions. However, having a critical situation forced upon them that requires them to think and quickly react under pressure with out-of-their-control variables results in errors 80 to 90 percent of the time!

In police reports of fatal crashes involving at least one car carrying two or more teenagers, there is some evidence of the following distractions:[1]

- Turning to talk to someone in the back seat
- Engaging in risky maneuvers like passing another vehicle
- Physical interference like a passenger attempting to take control of the steering wheel

In order to drive safely, each driver needs to own the responsibility of recognizing when a distraction or set of distractions materialize. This is especially true for complex distractions. Understanding that attention will be diverted to manage a distraction helps a driver maintain situational awareness. Drivers have one large luxury over pilots. When driving a car, it is easier to pull over, suspend the trip, and manage the situation. By stopping the vehicle, the driver's attention can be completely refocused on solving the distraction while not having to simultaneously concentrate on the safe operation of a moving vehicle. This is a great strategy for breaking a negative trend. Instantly pulling an airplane over and suspending the flight is obviously not an option for pilots. They have to deal with the distraction(s) at least to the point when an emergency landing can be made, but even an expedited emergency landing could take several minutes or even hours if over a large body of water.

Preoccupation

Preoccupation is similar to day dreaming. You are preoccupied when you are thinking about an event in a different place and time from the present. Being preoccupied while driving can slow problem recognition and reaction time. While driving home, thoughts about the upcoming prom or last week's football game will keep the mind of a young driver engaged, forcing him to control the car and think about non-driving events. Often the concentration level spent on driving increases and decreases depending on the demand for needing to make immediate driving decisions. The mind will tend to wander with an increase in preoccupation during boring and repetitive tasks such as cruising down a highway.

With preoccupation, a driver still keeps the car on the road and drives along as he normally would, but complete attention is diverted from driving awareness and drifts between driving and day dreaming about non-driving related thoughts. The problem arises when an accurate driving decision is required when his mind is taking a turn at being heavily consumed in a day dream event. When this happens, an additional step is added to making a corrective action in that the driver must first snap out of day dreaming phase and become refocused on driving before trying to process a driving threat.

Preoccupation often happens during the mundane and boring parts of a trip when the requirement for other driving safety details are in low demand. Trying to think ahead and anticipate upcoming dangerous areas like intersections, merge lanes, and congested traffic might serve as a check point to determining the level of preoccupation. When one of these activities is approaching, a driver might recognize this as a need to take a quick mental inventory of what is going on and refocus on the upcoming event.

Absorption

Becoming too absorbed or fixated on a particular task will tend to divert attention away from managing the several important tasks needed to complete a driving trip by focusing attention on a subset of the tasks. Having a casual conversation with a passenger, while concentrating on making safe driving decisions, happens all the time with drivers and does not pose a huge safety threat. When a casual conversation becomes more intense and requires more focus from the driver, it may become a distraction and the driver might ask the passenger to stop for a moment while the driver manages a driving issue. If, however, the driver becomes totally absorbed in a conversation and turns to talk to the passenger for long periods of time (thus neglecting to scan for traffic and upcoming traffic signals that driver is absorbed in the conversation), the driver is neglecting other safety considerations and is dangerous.

Absorption and fixation concepts are taught to pilots, especially to pilots going through instrument training. If a pilot fails to scan all relevant instruments when making flying decisions they expose themselves to two dangers. The first danger is by focusing on a subset of all important instruments; they are not receiving and interpreting all relevant data. The second danger is that if they do focus on certain instruments that happen to be giving erroneous readings they will be reacting to data that does not reflect what is actually happening to the airplane. Good instrument pilots keep up a constant instrument scan to continuously check all relevant instruments and cross check their primary instruments with secondary instruments to make sure all relevant data that is gathered is verified as being accurate using secondary sources.

This scan rate is important for drivers. Instead of scanning an airplane instrument panel, drivers might scan forward, approaching side streets, upcoming intersections, side mirrors, blind spot mirrors, rearview mirrors and repeat. Anticipate what actions might be needed ahead and scan for multiple sources of input to determine the best action.

Absorption or fixation is the most common inattention danger that I personally have to manage after a long instrument flight requiring a landing in bad weather. Preoccupation rates second and distractions are third. To me, distractions are the easiest to deal with because once I recognize they exist and are diverting my attention I can usually turn them off or get rid of them.

For drivers, I think it is important to realize that any combination of distractions, preoccupation and absorption can occur at any time to jeopardize attention needed to make safe driving decisions. Parents can help enforce rules that will limit distractions for the new driver like riding with passengers, talking on a cell phone, and playing loud music while driving. Young drivers can be proactive in trying to recognize the onset of inattention and make efforts to stay focused on the tasks at hand which is safely driving their vehicle and concentrating on making safe driving decisions.

Review

Most major distractions will be obvious. Caution is warranted during multiple or compounding "not so obvious" and seemingly smaller distractions.

- Know that events existing within your participation POP zone are themselves a distraction. The driver who is thinking ahead will benefit from realizing that a situation can change quickly and even though distractions are manageable for now, they might become overwhelming in a few seconds given a sudden change in surroundings and compounding events.
- Dynamic surroundings, inexperience in identifying distractions, managing distractions, and having to make fast decisions are a recipe for being forced to make a bad decision. Younger drivers lack experience in driving with distractions.
- Young drivers carrying a cell phone should avoid using it while driving. Some cities are trying to make it illegal to talk on a cell phone while driving. Programming frequently-used telephone numbers and using a hands-free headset will significantly reduce cell phone-related distractions.
- Pilot habits that apply to distractions are competent cockpit resource management, being aware of compounding events, having situational awareness, proactively looking for trouble, and breaking the trend.

Chapter 13
Road Rage

Road rage and aggressive driving are two terms that seem to be used interchangeably. I believe a distinction needs to be made.

Aggressive driving is controlling a vehicle in a manner that creates a dangerous situation for both the driver and surrounding vehicles. Examples include tailgating, changing lanes unsafely, speeding, illegal passing, and cutting off other vehicles. These acts are both unsafe and inconsiderate and can often result in a legitimate and chargeable traffic offense.

Road rage, however, goes beyond aggressive driving, though aggressive driving can lead to road rage. Road rage goes beyond an inconsiderate and dangerous traffic offense as it is a violent personal act and often with the intentions of causing bodily harm. Road rage attacks are criminal in nature. Extreme cases result in victims being shot, stabbed, and assaulted with tire irons, baseball bats, and large tools.

Both aggressive driving and road rage are threats to any driver. Law enforcement agencies have started education and awareness programs for drivers. The media has recognized the interest in these two topics and is also increasing drivers' awareness of the problems. Increased awareness is a good thing and will help drivers understand and manage their own behavior in order to avoid committing these acts. Avoiding road rage in oneself is just as important as recognizing and avoiding another driver who is threatening you. Both are situations that need to be identified and managed. See and avoid.

The National Highway Traffic Safety Administration has reported that the number of vehicles on roadways (demand) is outpacing the construction of additional roads (supply). From 1970 to 2000 population increased about 23 percent. During these three decades, the number of drivers increased by 72 percent.[1]

Perhaps more significant is that the number of vehicles per household jumped by 143 percent. One-car households began to purchase multiple cars. The average family now owns and operates two automobiles. In addition, over this same time span, the number of women in the workforce commuting to and from jobs increased 59 percent, thus adding even more cars to the roads.[2]

With these growth factors, the number of miles driven since 1987 has increased about 35 percent while the number of roads constructed has increased by only one percent. In addition to all of this, personal schedules are becoming busier and people too often feel the need to always get to the next event in a hurry.

Aggressive Driving

Traffic congestion is on the rise with no immediate relief in sight. Congestion will continue to increase. The individual driver has no control over the automobile population and congestion. Some of the main contributing factors leading to both aggressive driving and road rage are:[3]

- Traffic congestion
- A hectic and demanding personal time schedule
- More hours of the day being consumed with commitments leaving less time for commuting

Assuming that aggressive driving leads to many dangerous confrontations between drivers, it is important to highlight some of the more commonly agreed-upon situations that a driver might consider as aggressive in nature:

- Tailgating
- Illegal passing (double yellow or on the shoulder)
- Making rude or offensive gestures
- Failing to yield with merging traffic
- Flashing lights while directly behind another vehicle
- Cutting in line or delaying the merge to get out of a lane that is closing
- Blocking other drivers from merging in an orderly manner

Drivers who drive aggressively tend to have two characteristics.[4] First, they seem to be competitive in nature; that is, they like to compete and they see driving as an extension of "the game." They are aggressive in their everyday driving. Stunts like illegal passing to get around "the competitor" and crashing through a red light in an attempt to reduce the overall commute time are, in their eyes, a competitive win.

They rationalize these behaviors as necessary for "improving their score" or "setting a new record."

Second, many aggressive drivers feel they are doing nothing wrong. Aggressive behavior to them is normal operating procedure and they begin to drive even more aggressively when encountering a driver or other hindrance that slows them down.

In addition, drivers who have high anger levels also tend to drive aggressively. In fact, highly angered drivers tend to be twice as likely to participate in risky actions like drinking and driving, speeding, driving without seatbelts, and being inconsiderate to others.[5] Aggressive drivers often will commit multiple violations when trying to make up time or get ahead of other drivers.[6]

Pilots like to have full situational awareness and will immediately focus on anything that appears to deviate from the norm. Similarly, situational awareness and early detection of problems by younger drivers is perhaps the best defense against aggressive drivers. See and avoid. Recognizing aggressive driving behavior(s) and understanding that many of these aggressive drivers believe the manner in which they are driving is acceptable will better prepare younger drivers to develop and execute an out strategy.

When flying, I like to try and learn new things. One thing for sure, however, is that I avoid thunderstorms at all cost. They are extremely dangerous to aircraft. Studies and accident reports confirm a storm's ability to shred an airplane with just turbulence, let alone microbursts (sudden strong downdrafts), tornados, hail, lightning, and ice. I see and I avoid. I like finding aggressive drivers early and then get out and stay out of their way. See and avoid. As much as I like to compete, it is not worth the hassle or increased risk to dabble in such a meaningless game.

Aggressive drivers and those experiencing road rage are participants in your environment. They lurk and linger in your participation zone and might choose to target you. Think of these types of drivers as thunderstorms: They are unpredictable and capable of severe damage. Early detection and avoidance is the best strategy.

Spotting Aggressive Drivers

Spotting aggressive driving is usually fairly easy when a driver is vigilant about maintaining situational awareness. Quite often, one can detect the aggressive practices of another driver by either seeing their activity while following behind them or seeing their activity in side and rearview mirrors as they approach from the rear. Aggressive actions like cutting off cars and hazardous passing are easy to spot due to their erratic movement.

An interesting study published by the U.S. Department of Transportation looked at aggressive driving habits and how non-aggressive and aggressive drivers reacted to these events. The study noted that "aggressive drivers are often competitive." The study asked participants how often they got angry, became competitive, and/or became impatient in different driving situations. Aggressive drivers engaged in the following activities significantly more often than normal drivers:

- Blocking cars trying to change lanes
- Blocking cars trying to pass
- Drag racing at stop lights
- Competing with other cars in congested traffic
- Feeling impatient when the car ahead slows down
- Passenger tells driver to calm down

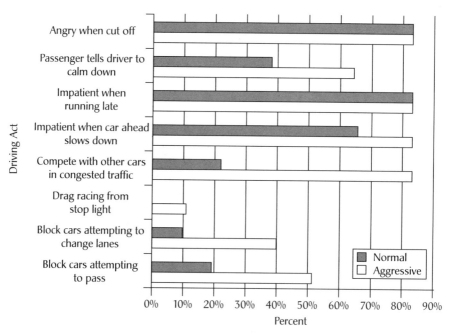

Aggressive and Competitive Drivers
National Highway Traffic Safety Administration. *Aggressive Drivers Are Often Competitive*. Washington, D.C.: National Highway Traffic Safety Administration, 1998.

Exhibiting Aggressive Driving Behavior

But what about the non-aggressive driver, the normal everyday driver who usually does not drive aggressively? I suppose everyone has a breaking point—a point at which they become angry and decide to take action against being pushed around. Through a series of events, the usually safe driver can find herself frustrated, aggravated, and challenged. She might start to "morph" into a retaliatory, aggressive driver. It happens to many drivers who normally are non-aggressive in nature. Perhaps after having a bad day, they quickly flip over into an aggressive driving mode. Even drivers who normally are not highly angry or overly competitive can fall into the aggressive driving mode.

Two common situations in which both normal and aggressive drivers have a high likelihood of becoming impatient, angry, and increasing their driving intensity are when they are behind schedule or when they are cut off by another driver. Younger drivers who are cognizant of these two scenarios will increase their awareness and help to prevent themselves from moving into an elevated driving intensity. In addition, they will better recognize aggressive drivers, thus seeing sooner and avoiding more quickly.

Being behind schedule is for the most part a situation over which a driver has control. Like some pilots, get-there-itis may set in and compound the pressure to make up time and perhaps drive a bit more aggressively than normal. Leaving earlier and allowing some time for congestion and delays should help reduce this situation. Being cut off by other drivers is a factor that many drivers will eventually have to deal with, but thinking ahead and anticipating these events should help minimize the occurrences of being confronted.

Road Rage

An increasing number of drivers have started to act out their aggression when behind the wheel, especially after being "provoked" by being tailgated or cut off by another vehicle. The AAA Foundation for Traffic Safety studied more than 10,000 incidents of violent, aggressive driving committed between 1990 and 1996 and found that at least 218 people were killed and another 12,610 were injured when drivers became angry.[7]

Many of these incidents involved male drivers between the ages of 18 and 26. However, any person can find themselves driving aggressively and then becoming further agitated. This may further compound a situation and transform aggressive driving into road rage with the desire to inflict personal harm.

There is not always a clear separation between aggressive driving and road rage. In fact, many studies do not distinguish between the two. Likewise, there is not always a clear progression of events that causes aggressive driving to cross the line and become road rage. You can be on the lookout for some common factors that can lead to road rage, but understand that the interaction between emotions and a wide variety of other variables is complex.

It is possible to be surprised by a violent driver on a mission to attack you. Say, for example, you cut off another driver, but do not realize you had done so. The other driver sees this as an aggressive act. You nonchalantly drive for a few miles. The other driver thinks you cut her off intentionally and that you are now ignoring her. She takes this as an act of spite and her adrenalin level skyrockets. Once you both slow down or stop at an intersection, the other driver leaves her car and confronts you. A very dangerous situation now exists and you did not even have a clue it had been unfolding over the past few minutes. In this situation, decision compression will squish anybody like a vise. What do I do? Where do I go? How do I escape? Do I confront and defend or flee? All these critical questions simultaneously converge on your brain as the other driver starts smashing your windshield with a tire iron.

I witnessed a similar scenario as a distant pedestrian at an intersection where one car caught up to another. The attacker was an extremely large man and the victim was a teenage girl. The man swerved in front of the girl at the intersection, blocking her in, and jumped out of his car with a tire iron. He proceeded to smash her windows and car. I later listened to police take her story while she shook uncontrollably—not from being injured, because she was never physically hit, but from pure terror. This was not in a big city but in a small, rural town on a country road. In the aggressive driver's words, the girl had "cut him off."

The following activities, while certainly inconsiderate, can also be considered aggressive, dangerous, and precursors to a road rage encounter.[8]

- Cutting off another vehicle
- Driving slowly (especially in the left "fast" lane)
- Tailgating
- Improper merging

It appears that most non-aggressive drivers seem to be okay with the aggressive driver going on their way and doing their own thing. They seem to have the mindset that, "Hey, if they want to injure themselves, then so be it, but leave me and other drivers out of it." If an aggressive driver commits an act that risks the well-being of other innocent and law-abiding drivers, the event could escalate the actions of all involved parties to an increased level of aggression.

If an innocent and non-aggressive driver has his personal space invaded and his well-being threatened by an aggressive driver, tensions are likely to escalate. The threatened non-aggressive driver may now have elevated frustration and perhaps an increase in adrenalin flow from a self-defense type of reaction. The possibility of retaliatory acts toward the aggressor is possible.

This seems to be one common example of aggressive driving escalating into road rage. When a driver aggressively responds to someone else's aggressive act, both drivers are in confrontation mode. The non-aggressive driver is making it known that she did not appreciate the encroachment into her space and the increased risk to her well-being. The aggressive driver is now intimidated and, since aggressive drivers often have competitive, risk-taking personalities, experiences an enhanced sense of aggression. The adrenalin flows and tensions rise.

A non-aggressive driver who responds to another driver's aggressive driving in any combination of the following responses increases the risk of causing the aggressive driver to cross the line into violent behavior.

- Making an obscene gesture
- Making direct eye contact
- Yelling or making facial expressions of anger or disgust
- Smiling, smirking, or other antagonizing gestures or remarks

Not responding to an initial aggressive act with action that may be perceived as aggressively retaliatory helps to keep many encounters rude and inconsiderate inconveniences rather than violent road rage incidents. It can be very difficult to not get caught up in the emotion and respond in an aggressive, retaliatory manner especially when your space and well-being are compromised by an "idiot." It is in this situation that younger drivers need to identify a potentially bad situation and take the opportunistic POP zone defense, electing to remove themselves from the situation. Remember: See and avoid, break the trend, and err to the conservative.

Consequences

As emotionally debilitating as it may seem to not respond to being pushed around, think of the consequences of responding and getting sucked into a very bad and potentially fatal scenario. Remember that studies indicate that the types of drivers who will invade your space are usually competitive in nature and will tend to have a hard time backing down from "a good confrontation." Many aggressive drivers also believe that their aggressive driving habits are completely acceptable to begin with. They feel you are nonstandard and are an idiot for not accepting their actions; this is an extremely volatile combination.

When it comes to aggressive driving and road rage, drivers can find themselves in two different situations. The first is when one becomes angry and frustrated and thus becomes the aggressive, retaliatory driver (personal POP zone). The second is when an aggressive driver starts to come after you (participation POP zone, then entering the opportunistic POP zone). There are different strategies for dealing with both.

You as the Aggressor

Should you become frustrated and agitated, the first step is to recognize this behavior shift and determine the root cause of the frustration. As we have seen, chances are you are running behind schedule and may be suffering from get-there-itis. To further compound the situation, a slower driver may be impeding your progress. The key here and the good news is that you are in control of your personal POP zone and can elect to not respond to the situation in a confrontational way.

Realizing that regardless of the events that have led to a particular scenario, whether in your control or not, you can elect how to deal with and manage the situation. Maybe an unexpected traffic accident or a mechanical problem caused you to fall behind schedule. It was your decision to leave when you did and not build extra time into the trip time for unexpected delays. If an event or series of events unfolds that put you behind, you just have to deal with it and come to the conclusion that things could be worse. More important, it is your decision as to whether things will deteriorate and become worse (compounding events) or if you will decide to manage the situation, stop it from compounding, and simply move ahead from there (break the trend).

Studies have shown that relaxation and visualization can reduce stress and anxiety. When your frustration level starts to rise due to traffic congestion and slow driving conditions, try the following five steps:

1. Blow out the air currently in your lungs. Then take a deep breath and hold it for five to ten seconds, at the same time think of all the things that are great in your life and that you really care about.
2. Fully blow all the air out again. As you exhale, envision blowing out all of the negative and frustrating feelings inside your body.
3. Take a deep breath and hold it for a short period of time while thinking about the fact that the roads are congested, everyone else is in a hurry, too, and even though you are getting frustrated, all of the drivers on the road are in the same situation.
4. Quickly visualize a volatile scenario whereby your actions lead to upsetting another driver to anger and having the situation compound into aggression and fighting.
5. Finally realize that a personal confrontation is just not worth it and that even though you may be late or behind schedule, it is better to get there in one piece a little late than not get there at all or have police paperwork and collision repair bills with which to deal.

You are in control and are responsible for managing the situation. Make like an electron and take the path of least resistance. Identify, manage, and avoid the unpleasant situation. When aggressive feelings start to emerge, another good initial response—and I emphasize initial response—to an aggressive act is to assume the aggressor is normally a calm and nice person and this aggressive behavior is abnormal for him. Assume he is having a bad day and give him a break. Taking this approach lets an aggressive driver do his thing and he will often shake his head in disgust or make a face, but will then continue on his way. If, however, an aggressive driver continues to be a threat, then abandon this approach and take any necessary action to protect yourself.

The Other Person as the Aggressor

The easy solution to the problem of aggressive driving is to recognize when other drivers are exhibiting aggressive driving tendencies and keep a close eye on them. Proactively manage your participation POP zone by keeping a high level of situational awareness. Simultaneously, start building your outs and determine how you will deal with the problem should it intensify.

Really, make your best efforts to avoid aggressive drivers entirely. Pilots are required to "see and avoid" other air traffic and are trained to anticipate problems. You need to anticipate and see and avoid other drivers' aggressive driving.

A confrontation with an aggressive driver will require a fast response. Note that your initial response to the situation will set the stage for how the aggressive driver will size you up as a competitor. When used in a retaliatory act, these previously mentioned responses tend to exacerbate the situation:

1. Making an obscene gesture
2. Making direct eye contact
3. Yelling or making facial expressions of anger or disgust
4. Smiling, smirking, or other antagonizing gestures or remarks

After a confrontation is encountered and your initial attempt to break the trend does not seem to extinguish the situation, then you are at a situational breaking point. Continuing with the confrontation will most likely cause the situation to deteriorate.

Let's say you are cool during an encounter with an aggressive driver. Even though you were not at fault and even though the aggressive driver threatened your safety by invading your space with their recklessness, you chose to ignore them and avoid further confrontation. This is a good start. However, if the aggressive driver continues to cut you off, flips you off, and remains a menace with no regard for your safety or for the safety of surrounding drivers, you now have a serious situation on your hands.

If this person has nothing better to do than go out of his way to continue to be a threat to you, then this should flash a big, bright red warning light. The second decision you make that will affect the outcome of the encounter is whether or not you allow the aggressive driver to take control of the situation and lure you into his game under his rules and engage in a road rage situation. Your decision at this point is whether to pull over, get out, and confront this aggression or flee, realizing that the situation is even more serious than previously thought. The question to answer is whether or not you want to continue being caught up in a situation with compounding problems that you do not have full control over. If the answer is "no," then break the trend.

The err-to-conservative decision is to try and remove yourself from the situation and flee. If you cannot flee or convince the aggressor to break it off, you must try and stay visible to other people and draw attention to yourself. Attempt to change the rules, so to speak, by taking control. Make it your "game" to break the trend and remove yourself from the situation. Also seek the assistance of other tools and personnel to make this event about you and not the aggressor. Some ideas to consider:

- Do not open a window or door. Do not make the aggressor's access to you any easier. Stay in the car and lock up. Let the aggressive driver see you get his license plate number and see you holding your cell phone if you have one. Make a call for help if you can. Even if your cell battery is dead, hold the phone up and let the aggressor see you dialing anyway. They will not know the battery is dead.
- When approaching a stop sign or intersection, try to avoid pulling up close to the vehicle in front of you. Being too close to the vehicle ahead of you allows the aggressor to pull in close behind you and block you in. If you leave 10 feet or so between you and the car in front of you (a larger-than-normal gap), you then maintain control, giving yourself room to pull out and around the car in front of you. This avoids allowing the aggressor to pin you in. Leaving a larger-than-normal gap builds you another out.
- Try to drive to a police or fire station to get leverage from professional safety personnel to help your cause. If you do not know where they are located, stay in view of other drivers and try to make it to a public place like a gas station or active parking lot. Do not pull into a parking space, though. Stay out in the open so you have the freedom to maneuver the car as an out strategy. Your goal is to recruit a team of bystanders to pay attention to your situation while keeping your 3,000-pound car surrounding you like personal body armor.
- Use your horn to make a scene and get the attention of others. This will clearly show the aggressor you are willing to defend yourself; the last thing he wants is witnesses to his aggressive acts or other people involved in defending you.

Review

- There is a difference between aggressive driving and road rage, but aggressive driving often leads to road rage. Both present a danger to drivers.
- Responding with what are perceived to be retaliatory acts toward an aggressive driver, such as gestures and mouthed words, usually just serves to exacerbate the situation.
- Aggressive drivers are usually competitive in nature and like to compete while driving.
- They also often feel that their aggressive driving behavior is acceptable and normal.
- There is usually a point at which the victim has the opportunity to break the trend during a situation deteriorating from an initial aggressive driving incident to violent road rage. Be on the lookout for this opportunity to break the trend and take it. Break the trend and remove yourself from the situation or seek help from others.
- Take some time to store in your cell phone the telephone numbers of the police, sheriff, and highway patrol offices in areas in which you frequently travel. Think ahead. In a panic, it is great to have the numbers at the touch of a finger because 911 does not always work when dialed from a cell phone.

Chapter 14
Adverse Weather

Fog

Fog is condensed water vapor in a cloudlike mass close to the ground. Fog limits or, in severe cases, prevents visibility. It is essentially a cloud you would normally see in the sky down at ground level. It comes about when the amount of moisture exceeds the atmosphere's ability to absorb it. This excess moisture remains visible and is comprised of very tiny suspended water droplets or moisture.

Humidity refers to the presence of moisture in the air. Relative humidity is a measurement of the actual amount of moisture present in the air as compared to or relative to the total amount of moisture that could be present in the air at that temperature. Dewpoint is a term that defines the temperature at which air can no longer hold any more water. When the temperature reaches its dewpoint, the air is considered to be saturated.

Weather reporting stations report data enabling a calculation known as the temperature/dew point spread. This report is given as two numbers; the current temperature and the temperature to which the air must cool in order for the atmosphere to be unable to absorb any more moisture.

For example, a temperature/dew point weather report of 73° F/66° F means the current temperature is 73° F and the dew point is 66° F. This, in turn, means that once the air temperature cools to 66°, the air will not be able to handle the moisture and fog will result. However, visible moisture or fog usually starts forming when this temperature/dew point spread is within 4° degrees. So, in our example, once the air cools to 70°, the temperature would be within the 4° degree range of the reported 66° dew point and fog is likely to begin forming.

Any time moisture is added to the atmosphere (e.g., during a rain shower) or any time the temperature drops (e.g., at sunset or darkness, or due to approaching weather systems), the likelihood of fog formation increases. A quick check of the weather and temperature/dew point spread before going out for the night will give a good idea of what the likelihood of fog should be. Say an early evening news weather report states the temperature/dew point spread as 73°/66°. Fog would not be likely to occur because the spread between these two numbers is greater than 4° F. If a driver was planning on driving that evening and into the early morning hours and it was predicted to rain, she might antipipate fog to develop during the early morning hours. Generally speaking, once darkness sets in and the sun stops heating the Earth's surface, the temperature is likely to decrease (other weather variables and factors excluded, though there are exceptions). Should it rain, additional moisture will be added to the air. Cooling temperatures combined with additional moisture increase the likelihood of fog and reduced driving visibility. These cooling and moisture changes are two compounding events.

Fog can be condensed and patchy. Patchy fog is usually greatly influenced by local topographical characteristics and wind. It is not uncommon to see local patchy fog in valleys and low-lying areas where the temperature might be that critical 1° or 2° cooler. Remember from third-grade science that cooler air sinks, so the cooler air will naturally sink into the valleys and depressions along the landscape. Places with little or no wind allow fog to take its natural course with just temperature changes. It is also not uncommon to see fog over rivers and bridges crossing rivers. Evaporation from water in a river adds moisture to the air near the river. Rivers are usually lower in the land, relative to the immediate surroundings, and thus could have cooler temperatures relative to the surrounding areas. These two factors combine to generate fog.

Fog can greatly reduce visibility and this presents a safety threat to drivers and surrounding cars. Reduced visibility means the amount of time a driver has to gather and process data, and then react to a dangerous situation is usually reduced. In addition, with limited visibility, drivers may have their options for reacting to a situation reduced because they cannot see their surroundings as clearly.

It is a natural precaution to slow down when visibility is reduced. Drivers detect something out of the ordinary and want to slow down for safety. This is a natural course of caution. Once a foggy area is encountered, a vehicle will more than likely decrease its speed. A vehicle behind the first vehicle, following into the same area of limited visibility, would also slow down but might still be traveling faster than the preceding vehicle. Once the second car catches up to the first, the visibility could be so reduced that by the time the second vehicle detects the tail lights or brake lights of the lead vehicle, there may not be enough time to avoid a collision. The result would be both vehicles grinding to a halt in an accident. Now that they are not moving at all, subsequent vehicles would quickly approach them and possibly collide with the stopped cars, thereby adding to the pile. This is commonly referred to as a chain-reaction collision.

Visible moisture in the form of precipitation usually reflects some light. The microscopic water droplets suspended in fog act as miniature mirrors that reflect some light from the headlights in many different directions. Fog has the double effect of reducing visibility because the amount of light shining forward through the fog is reduced and fog will most likely generate reflected glare back toward the driver. This is distracting and dangerous. When entering fog at night, low-beam headlight settings typically provide the driver better visibility because the light beam projects closer to the ground and slightly below a driver's direct line of sight.

Fog can ground a pilot and prevent a flight. But for driving, it is usually more of a nuisance. Prior to driving, in the evening, early morning, at night, during cooling temperatures, prior to rain, or any combination of these, make a quick check of the weather. This way, you will be anticipating visibility challenges and allow for extra separation between cars, slower reaction times, and other cars slowing to deal with the reduced visibility. Think ahead and anticipate. Giving yourself a few extra minutes of driving time should reduce the onset of get-there-itis.

Flash Floods

Many people are surprised to learn that flash floods are the leading cause of weather-related deaths in the United States. Drivers need to be aware of and respect the power of fast flowing water over a roadway. Have you seen any video news clips of drivers being airlifted from cars by a helicopter because they drove their car into a fast water current?

Annual deaths from flash floods exceed lighting strikes, the second highest cause of weather-related deaths, by nearly two times.[1] General flooding poses threats to people in the form of electrical shock, drowning, and toxic contaminations due to water levels rising over time. However, the majority of weather-related injuries are caused by flash floods as people get swept away in the strong water currents.

Flash floods result from a rapidly increasing amount of water being dumped onto the ground and the surrounding terrain's inability to absorb and manage it. Common causes of flash floods are rain intensity and duration. Intensity is the amount of rainfall and duration is how long the rain continues to fall. Large thunderstorms, slow-moving storms, back-to-back storm systems, and heavy rains from hurricanes and tropical storms can lead to heavy, intense rainfall with enough duration to cause a flash flood. Even a hurricane in Florida is capable of injecting enough moisture into the atmosphere to cause flash flooding in Ohio or Pennsylvania if other conditions are correct.

In addition to heavy storms, a broken dam or levee can also cause a rush of water leading to a flash flood. As a result of a break, these floods can happen within a few minutes and their power is impressive. Water running in a flash flood can rip out trees, move boulders, destroy buildings, and knock over bridges. Floating debris and sometimes ice are commonly found moving in a flash flood. They will cause additional damage by acting as battering rams when colliding with objects.

Flash floods present a hazard to drivers. More than one-half of all flash flood-related fatalities are automobile related.[2] Drivers have a hard time estimating the depth of the water encountered in a flash flood and they often underestimate its speed. In addition, the power of moving water is hard to comprehend for people—until they have experienced it. You need to know that it only takes six inches of fast-moving water to knock an adult off his feet and sweep him downstream. It takes only about two feet of fast-moving water to float and sweep a car away. Many people do not realize these facts and try to drive through flash flood water thinking they can drive slowly and make it through.

Drivers faced with making decisions regarding flash flood waters often experience the following:

- They underestimate the water's depth, especially at night. They are often surprised to find that the water is deeper than expected.
- They fail to accurately estimate the power of the water's rapid current.
- They fail to plan for the fact that the water depth and current strength will continue to rise rapidly.
- They fail to anticipate that moving debris can hit them or their vehicle and cause substantial damage.

There is no correlation between a vehicle's weight and size to the safety it provides. Any vehicle can be swept away. Eighty percent of all flash flood fatalities are the result of drivers ignoring flash flood warning signs and trying to traverse flooded areas.[3]

Water weighs 62.4 pounds per cubic foot and will, on average, flow at a rate of 6 to 12 miles per hour. When a vehicle is stopped in water, the momentum from the moving water is transferred to the car. For each foot of water depth, approximately 500 pounds of lateral force is applied to the car. In addition to lateral force, the buoyancy of the car also is a compounding factor. For each foot of water depth, the car will displace 1,500 pounds of water. This, in effect, causes the car to weigh 1,500 pounds less for each foot of rising water.

Two feet of flood water means a car is displacing 3,000 pounds of its own weight and the same two feet of moving water applies 1,000 pounds of lateral force. This explains why just two feet of moving water will sweep away most automobiles and highlights the main reason drivers get into trouble. These factors contribute to the 80 percent of flash flood fatalities who are drivers. Flash flood water, less than two feet deep, swept away and carried a 46,000 pound cement truck in Los Angeles.[4]

If the water current does not sweep the car away, drivers who try to cross flooded areas will usually get into water deep enough to stall the engine, causing them to sit helpless while the water level and current continue to intensify to a level capable of washing a car and its occupants downstream. Experts say that if a car stalls in rapidly rising water, the occupants should abandon the vehicle and seek higher ground.[5]

Remember that it takes less than six inches of fast-moving water to sweep a person off of her feet. Trying to escape by wading through flash flood currents or being trapped in a stalled vehicle caught in flash flood water will be a dangerous situation. Remaining in the vehicle puts a driver at risk of being hit by moving debris in the water, rising water levels, increasing water current speed, and being swept away. If trapped, chances are the intensity will continue to rise at a surprisingly fast level so try to get out of the vehicle before the water rises.

The best advice is to see and avoid flash flood areas. It does not necessarily have to be raining in an area for a driver to encounter flash flood waters. Water from heavy rains at a higher elevation in a surrounding area will find its way downhill and can flow into areas where rain is not present. Increase your situational awareness and think two steps ahead during storms. Not only does being trapped in a flash flood put you at risk, it also puts your would-be rescuers at risk. Approximately one-half of all swift-water drownings are either well-trained rescue personnel or good Samaritans feeling the need to attempt a rescue.[6]

In addition to driving through flood waters, drivers should also be aware that crossing a bridge that is above flood currents will still put them a risk. Studies show that nearly one-third of bridges and flooded roads are structurally unstable and present safety hazards.[7]

Summer

Summer driving in most areas in the country means heat. Cars operate differently due to external weather and environmental variables. Driving in the heat of summer means that an already hot-running engine must now function within hot surroundings. It is important to keep the engine coolant at the proper level. Engine coolant is more than just water; it is a mix of water and a coolant specially blended to assist in cooling a hot engine block. Water boils at a relatively low temperature compared to the heat generated from a car engine and by itself is not capable of cooling. A mix of water and engine coolant raises the boiling point and thus helps to cool the engine by dissipating heat. In addition, the proper amount of fresh motor oil provides better internal lubrication and will assist in reducing the frictional heat of moving engine parts.

If you must keep a car parked and running for a while in the heat of summer, it is usually a good idea to open the hood to allow additional heat dissipation. When a car engine is running but not moving, airflow moving over the engine is limited and cooling ability is reduced. Opening the hood allows some heat to rise and escape.

Lightning

During the spring and summer, thunderstorms, lightning, hail, and tornados can present driving hazards. Most of these occur suddenly, leaving the driver and passengers little time to react.

A powerful thunderstorm can produce each of these weather phenomena and they can be nasty and dynamic. Intense thunderstorms have killed many pilots who got too close to them. In fact, the FAA requires that aircraft stay at least 20 nautical miles away from thunderstorms due to their destructive capabilities.

The government issues both weather watches and weather warnings for flooding, severe thunderstorms, tornados, and high winds. A weather watch is an alert making people aware that the conditions are right for the possible formation of a weather system. Therefore, a tornado watch indicates that the conditions are right for a tornado to form. Weather warnings are more critical than watches. A tornado warning means that either a tornado has been spotted by a properly trained weather observer or a radar system has plotted echo signatures that are associated with tornados. Warnings mean that you should react immediately. While driving, especially on long trips, it is a good idea to keep your situational awareness high and stay abreast of weather changes. Radio stations will usually broadcast severe weather information so when the sky starts to look threatening, start scanning the channels.

When lightning flashes, drivers can still hear short bursts of static if they have the AM band of a radio tuned in. This is a trick pilots started using many years ago, prior to today's more sophisticated radar and navigation systems. By tuning their low-frequency ADF (Automatic Direction Finding) equipment to a local AM broadcast station, they would listen for static "pops" or crackling static noise on the radio, indicating that lightning was near. Lightning is generated by a thunderstorm.

A single bolt of lightning may contain up to 100 million volts of electricity and can be as hot as 50,000 degrees—hotter than the sun's surface. This is extremely concentrated energy, capable of tremendous damage. The good news for drivers is that being inside a metal car during lighting is actually a relatively safe place to be.

One misconception many people have is that cars are safe from lightning because the tires insulate the vehicle from the ground. This is inaccurate. It is not the tires that provide the added safety but rather the car's metal frame. Electric currents from lightning are mostly channeled and carried on the outside of conducting objects. This phenomenon is called skin effect. This holds true for metal vehicles. When lightning strikes a car, most of its electrical current passes around the outside of the vehicle as long as the car frame is made of metal. Most car bodies are made from metal and therefore make a good shelter from lightning. Corvette and Saturn car bodies are not entirely metal; they contain fiberglass, which is a poor conductor of electricity.

While inside a car during a lightning strike, drivers and passengers should:

- Have the windows fully closed.
- Turn the car ignition off and sit with hands folded on their laps. Touching the steering wheel, gas or brake pedals, or any

part of the car frame is dangerous because it puts you in closer contact with the conducting metal during a strike. Shoes will help insulate you from the car's floorboard but quickly rolling or folding the floor mat and then placing your feet on top of the mat is a good idea.

• Do not talk on a cell phone or a CB radio that is connected via a powercord to the cigarette lighter socket or connected to an external antenna cable. In addition, do not hold onto a cord or any device that is connected to the car frame via a cord. Any device requiring power from a car's electrical system will be electrically connected to the frame. This includes electronic devices such as a personal CD or cassette tape player using the cigarette lighter as a power source. Electricity will travel through these wires.

Keep most cars in mind as a relatively safe shelter from lightning as long as windows and doors are shut and occupants are not touching metal objects connected to the car's frame. It makes a great destination to run to during Junior's little league game.

Tornados

Tornados come in all shapes and sizes. They happen at daytime and at night. They can be easy to spot and clearly definable or they can hide within large clouds of dust and debris or in the darkness of night.

Tornados are classified in intensity from F0 to F5. Tornados with an F0 classification have winds in the 40 to 72 miles per hour range. F5-ranking tornados can have winds ripping along at over 300 miles per hour!

Unlike during a lightning strike, being inside an automobile when a tornado is threatening is usually unsafe. A car can be blown over, tumbled across the ground, or even sucked up into the tornado's vortex to be eventually spit out several hundred feet away. I like to use the analogy that sitting in a car during an approaching tornado is like being a kernel of popcorn about to be popped inside of a hot-air popcorn popper.

Tornados and automobiles is a bad combination, so the goal is to avoid the confrontation by avoiding the bad weather area or leaving the car for better shelter. Monitoring weather reports and visually scanning the sky are good starters. When a tornado is on the ground, it sucks up and spews out dirt, mud, water, vegetation, homes, telephone poles, bricks—anything and everything in its path. This destructive activity often creates tremendous debris clouds and can make the actual tornado hard to see. Low-bowl clouds floating close to the ground can also contain strong destructive winds. Flying debris is a secondary treat to bystanders besides the brut wind force. While inside a car during a tornado, drivers and passengers should:

- Do not try and outrun a tornado. They have been clocked moving in excess of 60 miles per hour along the ground. Although a driver could get a car moving over this speed, the surrounding confused drivers, congested traffic, and impaired visibility would most likely hinder and slow the escape attempt.
- Be aware that tornados' paths are extremely erratic and they often change directions many times without notice.
- Get out of the car and seek shelter in a building, a culvert, or a ditch, all of which are preferable to remaining inside a car.
- Watch for tons of debris flying out from a tornado. Debris can range in size from small splintered glass to railroad boxcars. All can be hurtled some distance from the actual tornado.
- Recognize that tornados often occur near the trailing edge of a thunderstorm or storm front.
- Know that before a tornado hits, the surrounding air may become very still with calm winds.

Driving in Wet Weather

According to National Highway Traffic Administration statistics, approximately one million motor vehicle accidents occur annually in wet weather. Many drivers fail to recognize that there is a significant difference between driving on dry and on wet road conditions.

Heavy rain can often cause flash flooding and can also severely limit driving visibility. Drivers encountering heavy rain, especially when in unfamiliar driving environments, tend to slow down and continue at a slower speed. Similar to driving in fog, driving at a slower speed is okay as long as all drivers adjust to the lower speed. Cars moving at different and slower speeds mean that separation gaps between vehicles are reduced.

Any time there is standing water on the road, a car may hydroplane. Hydroplaning occurs when the car's tires cannot channel all the water through the grooves in the tire tread and thus some water remains under the tire. With a layer of water between the road surface and the tire, there is an instable surface that will promote skidding and sliding. In general, all-weather tires are designed to channel water better than higher-performance tires. Bald or worn tires will be more susceptible to hydroplaning. Proper tire inflation will help the tires' ability to channel and displace water. Reduced driving speed and following in the tire tread path of preceding cars should improve traction.

Tire Conditions

Appropriate tire tread depth and proper tire inflation encourage safe driving by improving braking action, maneuverability, and a driver's ability to move through water and snow. Tread grooves channel water and allow it to quickly flow from underneath the tires up and behind the tires as the car moves forward. A recent automotive survey indicated that 70 percent of American drivers do not know how to determine if they have sufficient tread depth on their tires.[8]

A simple test is to place a penny right-side up into a tire's tread grooves. If part of Lincoln's head is covered by the tread, then more than 2/32-inch tread depth remains. This is usually the absolute minimum acceptable tread depth.

The same survey indicated 86 percent of drivers do not check their tires for proper inflation. Under inflation hinders tires' ability to channel water. In addition, under inflated tires will reduce the performance of the vehicle when turning, stopping, or otherwise controlling the car. Information about a tire is usually imprinted on the tire itself and can generally be found printed on the outside of the tire near the hubcap area or wheel. Proper tire inflation information is often in this area. Use a tire inflation gauge to measure the current tire pressure and then inflate or deflate the tire to meet the recommended inflation.

Heavy Rain and Hail

Thunderstorms are extremely turbulent. The collision of rain droplets and the friction caused by millions of raindrops rubbing together actually generate the electricity to form lightning. As raindrops continue to collide and merge, they grow in size.

Thunderstorms can exceed 50,000 feet in height. At these higher altitudes, the water droplets are cooled down and freeze. Even though it may be a pleasant 65° on the ground, it may be −60° at 50,000 feet. Hail is formed by freezing rain droplets. When hailstones repeatedly collide with additional water droplets, they refreeze and grow in diameter. When hail is lifted and finally ejected out of the upper part of a thundercloud, it rapidly falls to the Earth's surface before it has a chance to melt. Hail is a good clue that you are in the vicinity of a nasty storm system.

Hail can range in size from a pea to a baseball. It sometimes falls to Earth at such size and speed that it can kill people and cause severe damage to vehicles. Hail can easily shatter a windshield. If a driver encounters large hail, it is best to park the car under something such as an overpass or a bridge or in a garage for protection.

While inside a car during heavy rain and hail, drivers should:

- Maintain a safe distance from vehicles in front of them. It takes longer to stop on a wet road surface than it does a dry surface, even with good wet-weather tires.
- Expect drivers in front of them to slow down or even stop in their traffic lane.
- Slow down. As vehicle speed decreases, the tire footprint (the amount of the tire's tread touching the road surface) increases and this improves the tire's ability to channel water. This, in turn, provides for improved stopping distance and controllability.
- If driving in an area which often experiences wet-weather conditions, consider equipping the car with tires manufactured with a wet-weather tread design and rubber compounds.
- Make smooth driving adjustments and avoid abrupt changes in direction or speed.
- Avoid hydroplaning. If a driver feels the vehicle begin to behave sluggishly and start to slide or not react to the controls, he should take his foot off the accelerator first before braking.
- Use fast windshield wiper speeds.
- Be prepared to pull over and wait it out.
- Watch out for standing water.
- Stop driving and pull over during hail and if possible, park under a protective barrier.

Winter

Winter flying presents significant challenges for pilots, especially for pilots of smaller aircraft that lack some of the more sophisticated avionics and anti-icing/deicing systems. Ice, poor visibility, and cold weather operations are especially challenging for pilots. Many of the winter hazards present for pilots also exist for drivers.

Heavy Snow

Heavy snow severely reduces driving visibility. Similar to fog, snowflakes reflect light and reduce visibility; snow is a double compounding problem—reduced visibility and slippery roads combine to make especially treacherous driving conditions. Drivers will usually have better visibility in heavy snow when using a low-beam headlight setting. This reduces the amount of glare from the snowflakes.

Snow accumulation makes roads slick as it builds a layer of slippery moisture between the tires and the road's surface. Drivers can then experience hydroplaning, resulting in a car that is difficult to handle.

With weather, temperature means everything, especially in the range of 32° F plus or minus 2°. Road conditions are dynamic and ever changing. In a given short stretch of road, a driver might encounter road surfaces with no ice, but merely slush. The road surface temperature then might decrease a degree but because the road is heavily traveled, the friction-heated road, along with salt or chemical treatments, may keep the water from freezing. Exiting from a highway onto a side street with a lower traffic volume or trying to stop at the bottom of an exit ramp may prove difficult because the surface might now be cooler and at or below freezing. A nearby bridge might have a temperature of 28° since; the air blowing above and underneath the bridge rapidly cool the structure. All of these factors change and affect driving conditions in a short period of driving distance, perhaps in just a mile.

Freezing Rain

Freezing rain can devastate flying aircraft and road surfaces. Moisture is capable of staying in liquid form even when the temperature drops below freezing. This is confirmed by observing a stream of water flowing along when the outside temperature is substantially below freezing. If water is moving or "jiggling," it maintains surface tension and stays a liquid even when the temperature is below freezing. As long as the surface tension remains undisturbed, moisture may remain in liquid form even though the surrounding temperature may be substantially below freezing,

Clouds at temperatures below freezing often contain raindrops. As the water drops are bounced around inside the cloud, their constant movement keeps them from freezing. Raindrops that are below freezing temperatures are known as super-cooled water drops. These super-cooled drops remain as a liquid until their surface tension is disturbed or broken. While in the cloud, an airplane wing hitting these super-cooled drops at a few hundred miles per hour instantly disturbs their surface tension and because the water drops are already below freezing, they instantly freeze upon contact with the wing, propeller, windshield, landing gear, or any part of an airplane's structure.

Super-cooled raindrops can remain in liquid form until they hit the road's surface. As when they collide with an aircraft wing, these drops instantly freeze upon contact with a car or road surface. This is known as freezing rain. Larger storm clouds can drop a significant amount of freezing rain in a short amount of time.

Freezing rain covers everything and turns into heavy and slippery ice. Even small amounts of freezing rain can have substantial weight. Tree branches break, power lines snap, and roads become covered with a layer of ice. Road ice from freezing rain can make it challenging to maintain control of a vehicle. The best strategy here is avoidance.

Icy and wet road conditions have a big impact on braking performance and stopping distance. Pilots receive braking action reports when approaching to land on runways that have had heavy rain or have icing conditions. Stopping a moving vehicle over ice may require a stopping distance of up to nine times greater than that needed to stop on a dry road surface.

Black Ice

Black ice is different from freezing rain. It is caused when moisture, usually suspended in the air, comes in contact with a cooler road surface. That surface further cools the moisture to below freezing. Thus a thin layer of ice is formed.

Black ice is often harder to detect than freezing rain. The ice, which is not really black, is called black ice because the black color of the road surface easily shows through the thin layer of clear ice. Road surfaces containing black ice may appear to shimmer as though wet, but in general, black ice is not easy to detect until a driver has spun out on it. If the temperature is at freezing and the road shimmers, look to see if surrounding cars have water spinning off of their tires. If not, then this is a good indicator that the road is not wet with water but instead is covered with a thin ice layer.

Black ice can form at any time, but expect it late at night or early in the morning when the temperature may be low. In addition, because roads are typically less traveled at these times, frictional heat from tires is reduced, providing an enhanced freezing environment for a road's surface.

Freezing Surfaces

Temperature rules the weather kingdom. One degree of temperature variance can mean the difference between standing water or ice. Because bridges have a dual cooling characteristic—they are cooled from the top on the road's surface as well as underneath by wind blowing under the structure—their temperatures can drop below that of the road leading up to and away from the bridge. Because their surface temperatures often are lower, they tend to form ice sooner than the surrounding road surface. Beware of freezing road surfaces on bridges especially when temperatures are right around the magical freezing mark of 32° F. This phenomenon also can occur when it is windy.

A misconception that some drivers have is that ice is more slippery as temperature decreases. This suggests that some drivers believe that driving over ice at temperatures near the freezing level is somewhat safer than driving over ice when the temperature is well below freezing.

Tires again play a large part in winter driving. The following characteristics are important to note:

- **Tire design.** The material of which a tire is made is important because different polymer compounds react differently in cold weather. Some tire materials may get extremely hard and slick in freezing temperatures, more so than some all-weather tires might. All-season tires are comprised of several compounds that are combined to enhance tire wear and life. However, the trade-off is that once the temperature drops below 50° Fahrenheit, their traction is reduced. Tires designated as "Winter" can have traction increased from 25 percent to 50 percent over all-season tires and their cold weather handling capabilities are superior.
- **Tread design.** Tread gaps enable snow and water to be lifted and channeled from underneath the tire. All-weather tires tend to do a better job of channeling snow and water than say high-performance tires designed for warm weather and dry roads.

- **Tire inflation.** Properly inflated tires are important for maximum performance. An under-inflated tire lets more of the tire's surface sag and make contact with the road. This reduces the tire's ability to channel away water and snow.

Review

- The number-one error drivers make in adverse driving conditions is failure to adjust their speed relative to conditions. They often drive too fast. Stopping distances can stretch to about nine times that of stopping distances on dry roads.
- Increase vehicle separation—at least triple the distance you would maintain in normal conditions.
- A car is usually a safe place to be during lightning but is relatively unsafe during high winds or tornados.
- Road conditions constantly change, even over a short distance, so the conditions experienced a mile back might well not be the condition encountered a mile ahead.
- Ice is slippery at any temperature but is usually more slippery when the temperature is close to the freezing level.

Chapter 15
Safely Approaching
Your Vehicle

Prior to taking off, good pilots usually complete both a preflight planning process and an aircraft walk around to verify if the aircraft is worthy of safe flight. In preflight, pilots usually plot a desired course, research the destination airport, check the weather, and determine if an alternative landing destination might be needed due to weather. The walk around is the physical inspection pilots give the plane prior to loading passengers, starting the engines, and taking off.

Preflight is a critical step because it is here you can detect potential problems such as low tire pressure, malfunctioning aircraft components, bird nests in the engine cowling, bee nests in the air vents, and so forth. Obviously it is easier to deal with these situations while on the ground.

Vehicle Walk Around

Automobiles are less complex and easier to check over than aircraft. If a moving car starts making a strange noise or a front wheel starts to shimmy, drivers can quickly pull off the road, get out, and inspect the situation. While airborne, pilots simply do not have this luxury; they cannot just pull over and get out to check a suspicious noise. I have learned over the years to take advantage of the luxury of being able to pull my automobile over while driving to check out something suspicious.

To check all the systems and components of an aircraft, even of a small single-engine airplane, can take several minutes. Approaching a vehicle and completing a walk around is not much different than doing so for an aircraft—it's just easier and much faster. In fact, a good portion of a car's walk around can be completed while walking toward the vehicle. This takes little time and helps to ensure nothing is overlooked.

Take a quick walk around the car to check for:

- Suspicious strangers near your vehicle
- Fluid dripping under the front of the car (coolant, fuel, oil, or brake fluid) and under the rear of the car (fuel or brake fluid)
- Broken or damaged mirrors, headlights, or tail lights
- Headlights and taillights that are clean and free of dirt and/or dust
- Secure and clear tailpipes and exhaust system
- Tires that appear to be properly inflated
- Latched trunk and hood

Once inside the car, immediately lock the doors and start the engine. Then complete your "preflight" or "pre-drive" checklist:

- Verify that no one is threatening your safety by approaching the car.
- Make sure that the seat is correctly positioned.
- Check that the mirrors are set properly for your posture and field of view.
- Confirm that all engine warning lights check out okay.
- Make sure the amount of fuel is adequate. Determine if a stop at a gas station is needed.
- Ensure that all passengers are secure with seat belts fastened.
- Make sure the interior is secured from flying objects should there be a sudden stop.
- Confirm that the outside surroundings are clear.

I often travel and rent cars at destination cities. This pre-drive ritual evolved over the years because I needed to get familiar with the various rental cars all with different settings and control locations. As I approach the rental car, I make sure there is a license tag, tires, lights, and that the car body is fine and dent free. I also determine what side of the car the fuel cap is on so I know what side to park next to the pump for refueling. Once inside, I lock the door. In just a minute or so, I familiarize myself with and test the wipers, lights, and door lock features. I test the turn indicators and finally I adjust both the rearview and side mirrors. I have eliminated several driving distractions because I already know how the equipment works. It's the pilot in me—always thinking two steps ahead.

Carjacking

Even prior to determining if there are any noticeable mechanical problems with your car, the act of approaching your vehicle should be considered. Unfortunately, society contains criminals who are destructive in nature and prey on individuals. Carjackings and abductions pose a threat to all people. Younger drivers need to be aware that either of these calamities can occur at any time, whether while approaching their vehicle in a parking lot at night or creeping slowly through congested traffic.

Carjacking refers to a theft in which a motor vehicle is taken by force or the threat of force. Carjackings started to escalate in the 1980s.[1]

They are a violent form of vehicle theft and can present a life-threatening situation to any driver or passenger. While stealing the vehicle, carjackers sometimes kidnap the driver or pull the driver from the car and escape with the other occupants still in the vehicle. Drivers who are not prepared for this life-threatening assault will most likely encounter instant and overwhelming decision compression and panic.

Auto theft is a big business. Numerous reports confirm that over one million cars are stolen each year in the United Sates. With today's sophisticated auto theft alarms, engine cut-off circuitry, and ignition keys embedded with microchip technology, it makes sense that thieves seek to and will benefit from stealing a car that is already running.

There is a higher street value for a car that has not had the window glass or steering column broken and on which the ignition wires are still intact. In addition, carjackings usually can be accomplished much more quickly than breaking into and hotwiring a car, thus providing a quicker escape for the thief.

The U.S. Department of Justice completed a special report on carjackings using data collected from the National Crime Victimization Survey (NCVS) for the years 1992 through 1996. It was reported that an average of 49,000 carjackings occurred in the United States in each of those years.[2]

In addition, the following statistics were reported for that same time period:

- About 50 percent of carjacking attempts were completed.
- 92 percent of carjackings involved one victim.
- 83 percent of carjackings involved a weapon.
- 65 percent of successful or attempted carjackings occurred within five miles of the victim's home. Some even occurred within the victim's own garage.

- 62 percent of victims took some kind of action to defend themselves.
- 34 percent of victims used no confrontational forms of defense like calling for help or running away.

Carjackings can often occur in busy commercial areas where cars are parked and there is ample entering and exiting activity occurring around the parked cars. Most carjackers want the keys and the car. The element of surprise is important to carjackers and helps to startle the victim who is entering or exiting the vehicle. This is the classic set-up for decision compression followed instantly by panic and confusion.

In addition to carjackings, other violent crimes such as rape, robbery, and purse theft can occur around a person's vehicle. These assaults can and do occur to both drivers and passengers. In these instances, the assailant is not interested in the keys or the car but has other motives.

Given their choice, attackers will often choose:

- A victim they can surprise rather than a victim who might suspect an attack is starting to unfold.
- A victim who appears timid rather than a victim who appears confident.
- A victim who is awkward, clumsy, and disorganized rather than a victim who is organized and aware.

Victims who are jumped or surprised usually take longer to process the situation, evaluate their alternatives, and decide on an action plan. Therefore, they often panic and succumb to decision compression, giving their attackers the exact advantage they were initially seeking—a surprised victim who now has disorganized thoughts trying to quickly evaluate the threat and contemplate a reaction.

Situational awareness and thinking two steps ahead will help create a safer environment. It is amazing to me the number of people I observe who approach their vehicles without even thinking about their vulnerability or who fail to scan their environment for danger; they do not manage their participative POP zone.

While they are learning to drive, I encourage young drivers to discuss certain scenarios and courses of action with their parents. Build an initial action plan for a given situation and then if confronted, decide to execute the action as rehearsed or modify the action as needed given the specifics of the situation. Think two steps ahead by having a reaction plan and then an adjustment plan should you want to deviate. Confrontation with an attacker is a dangerous thing and one should think along the grounds that if a person is crazy enough to attack me that they are crazy enough to do anything.

Handling Confrontations
Run through some scenarios on how you would react if:

- You were alone and an attacker threatened you while approaching from a distance.
- You were alone and getting into your car when an attacker confronted you.
- You had a younger child with you and were confronted.

The responses might be different from person to person. There is no magical answer, but there is merit to quickly deciding on how you want to initially react and having a plan ready to execute at a moment's notice. Remember, the attacker is hoping you immediately get consumed with decision compression, panic, and falter in responding to the threat. The first sign of hesitation or confusion is usually the exact clue an attacker is looking for and will often confirm for them that they have found a weak target. This encourages them to continue the attack.

Perhaps you might decide that if an attacker threatens you from a distance, you will initially yell, scream, and start to run away. You then immediately validate your response by seeing how the attacker responds. If they do not pursue you, then your escape plan or out is working and you should continue fleeing. If, however, the attacker starts chasing you, perhaps you should decide to show them your car keys and throw them away from you and in the opposite direction from which the attacker is approaching. If possible, throw the keys behind the attacker as this will force him to stop approaching and turn to walk away from you if he wants to get the keys. Break the trend.

If you are opening your car door and an attacker surprises you, then pushes you into your car, and forces you to drive at knife point, you may decide to comply. Comply that is until the first opportunity to purposely wreck the car by running the attacker's side of the car into a pole or building and immediately jumping out of the car with nearby Samaritans who might come to your aid. Again there is no magical answer and every situation is different. I think the worst situation for any victim is being abducted and taken to a secluded place, where there are no potential rescuers.

Maybe with a child in tow, you decide to just give up the keys and not make a stand. I want to emphasize that there is no standard or consistently accurate retaliatory response. What might be a good strategy for one scenario could very well be a poor strategy for another.

The key point here is to discuss how you best want to handle these confrontations. If you are a nationally ranked black belt, your action plan will most likely differ from someone who is physically challenged. Walk through some of these scenarios and construct a few outs or responses to these situations. Have an initial plan ready to execute and then if it is put into action, be prepared to validate its effectiveness and deviate if necessary.

Verifying the Safe Vehicle

Verifying that your vehicle is safe becomes especially important when your vehicle is parked in a public place where people have easy access to the vehicle and its surroundings. Parking lots, shopping centers, convenience stores, banks and ATMs, restaurants, and hotels are popular areas for both carjackings and assaults.

We have all heard the police reports of people being abducted or assaulted while getting into their cars. I continue to see people coming out of a store or mall, waiting until they get next to their car before starting to dig for keys, opening their vehicle, and starting their engine. They then load their packages with their backs to an attacker's approach—with an opened car door and a running engine. Is there anything more inviting to a carjacker than the keys in the ignition, a running car, an open door, and the driver outside of the vehicle and not paying attention?

As you approach your vehicle whether in the dark or daylight:

- Take note of all the people around your vehicle, the path toward your vehicle, and the exit path you and your vehicle will use. Look around for signs of movement. Look for shadows of moving people if in a dark or poorly lit area. Better yet, do not park in a dark or poorly lit area.
- If there is water or snow, look for footprints that might belong to a person tampering with or stalking your car.
- Think about carrying a whistle. Whistles are standard equipment in survival kits because they generate substantial noise with a relatively small amount of air input.
- Have your door key in hand or the remote alarm ready to activate. Do not wait until you get to the door to fumble in search of the keys.

- Be cautious if there is a van or service truck parked near your car. They are great places for assailants to hide and wait until you are right next to your car and most vulnerable.
- Look under your car and the surrounding cars for a person hiding. You can do this while at a distance walking toward the car. You do not have to get right next to it and then bend over to check.
- As you get close to the car, look for abductors inside your car. Look to see if your windows have been tampered with or someone has attempted to gain entry.
- Anticipate an encounter while approaching your vehicle. This will make you more aware and cautious.
- Close and then lock the doors in order to restrict entry by unwanted individuals. Controlling your environment and your overall safety should be your top priority. By starting the engine, you are adding an additional element of safety by providing an improved way to make a faster getaway than if you had to fumble for keys and try to start the engine in a panic. Anticipate trouble and build your outs.

Managing an Assault While Driving

Intersections, especially those with stoplights, and roadways with easy access to a fast escape route provide a good opportunity for carjackers to take you by surprise. Whether parked in a lot or stopped at a light, the element of surprise greatly plays to the advantage of the carjacker. By sneaking up on the car, opening the door, and pulling the driver from the car, the event happens so fast that drivers are not prepared and have to think about how to react. Some instinctively flee, some instinctively fight back, and some panic and freeze.

In addition to attacking while you are stopped in traffic, carjackers sometimes will follow you and wait for a somewhat secluded area with a good escape route before attacking. Then they might slightly bump your car and gesture for you to pull over to discuss the "accident" that just happened.

Sometimes carjackers work in teams. One team method is for one car to bump you and convince you to pull over. Then a second car with two accomplices suddenly appears. One of them jumps out of the second car and into yours, making you either get out or drive away with the assailant in the car. In this case, there are two cars and three assailants.

In the above two scenarios, the carjacker's goal is to get you to stop moving, which increases your vulnerability, in a secluded witness-free place. If this happens, remember to keep your 3,000 pound suit of armor on. In other words, stay in the car with the doors locked and the windows closed. This provides an armored shield. Call for help or drive to a police station or a crowded area like a gas station. Criminals hate attention and they hate witnesses.

Anytime you have to stop at a light or intersection and there is a vehicle in front of you, stop soon enough to allow room to pull out and escape. If you pull up too close to the car in front of you, you have failed to create an out in that now you do not have room to pull out from behind the preceding car in an attempt to flee. Pulling up too close to a car in front of you allows an attacker's car to pull up to your rear bumper and block you in. Break the trend and think ahead. Plan your outs and leave that space between you and the car in front of you. This leaves you in control of executing an out.

Have an Action Plan

Determine a special word, phrase, or code that will instantly designate to your family members that a dangerous situation exists and that everyone is to immediately enter a defensive and protective mode. I especially encourage this exercise if younger children will be riding with a younger driver. This code word or phrase should signal to the child that what you say next is an instruction to be followed without delay and without question. In other words, just do it now and do it fast.

Say a driver is waiting to pick up a child from school. While parked front of the school or in a lot, an attacker quickly jumps into the car via the passenger door (because the driver failed to lock it) and is now holding the driver at knife- or gunpoint out of view from people outside the car. While the driver is trying to process this threat and figure out what to do, her child suddenly appears and starts to open the rear door to get into the car. An unprepared driver might suddenly tell the child to get out of the car. Children are curious and will often question "Why?" about 20 times in succession. They wonder why you are asking them to do something out of the ordinary routine. The last thing a driver needs in this situation is to get into a dialogue with the child on why she should not do what she normally does. The child's questioning of the non-standard instruction could jeopardize escape time and add to the potential chaos.

If, however, the driver and the child had previously agreed on a special danger code word and rehearsed an emergency plan, the driver could say the word, telling the child to run and get help. In theory, because the child knows this is the secret code for help or danger, she knows to react immediately without question or hesitation. Children are unpredictable, but having prepared them for just such a situation, they might actually remove themselves from the scene, get help for the driver, and potentially cause the assailant to think about fleeing now that help seems to be on the way. Having the ability to signal a threat to a friend or family member via a predetermined word or phrase is a powerful tool.

This is not a fail-safe method but the point is that being prepared and having some kind of action plan gives a person a starting point from which to make and adjust decisions. To increase the effectiveness of this strategy, it is important to review different situations with younger children and discuss how best to respond.

Review

- Attackers usually seek inattentive, timid, or clumsy victims. Proactively present yourself as someone who does not have these traits.
- Have some predefined action plans or outs ready to execute in certain situations. If confronted, immediately validate the plan's effectiveness and be willing and able to deviate based on the circumstances.
- Be attentive to your surroundings, both inside and outside your vehicle.
- Reduce your vulnerability by surveying your surroundings as you approach your car, looking inside to verify it is safe, unlocking the door, getting in, and immediately locking the doors and starting the engine. Then get situated.
- Devise and rehearse an emergency word or phrase to use with people you frequently travel with, especially younger children.

Chapter 16
Vehicle Control

Drivers of any age or experience level can lose control of their vehicle at any time. Ice, reckless drivers, mechanical failure, or driving too fast for the conditions can cause a vehicle to become uncontrollable, resulting in a crash.

Unfamiliar Roads

As with flying, the routine part of driving is fairly easy and somewhat boring especially if you fly or drive the same route day after day. Most of us have several driving routes we repeatedly traverse, from work, school, shopping, and so forth. A competency silo is built for each one of these trips and we quickly become comfortable and confident about making each individual trip. In fact, we usually do not even think about the trip itself.

Unfamiliar roads can catch drivers off guard and force them into immediate reactions, usually involving slowing down, or suddenly stopping. If moving too fast around a curve in the road, a decrease in speed is warranted to remain on the road.

Younger drivers should be aware that unfamiliar territory makes it more difficult to anticipate events and consequently requires longer decision processing and longer reaction times. Speeding, DUI, distractions, and adverse weather can all be events that compound and make negotiating an unfamiliar road even more dangerous. Increase situational awareness and anticipation when driving anywhere that is unfamiliar.

Rollovers

Forty percent of driving-related deaths occurring in 2001 involved vehicles rolling over.[1] Rolling a vehicle happened most frequently in crashes involving ditches, embankments, and culverts.

Taking turns too fast can cause drifting to the outside of the turn. Drifting too far to the outside of a turn can cause the front tire to slip off the edge of the road surface and onto the shoulder. Even though this might only be a few-inch drop, a moving car slipping off the road's edge usually startles drivers. Often the radius of the curve is inconsistent and if the radius is decreasing throughout the curve, the turn becomes sharper or tighter. This in turn requires the driver to increase the turn of the car. Higher speeds with sharper turns can lead to rolling a vehicle over. In 2001, 42 percent of roadside crashes occurred while driving around a curve.[2]

One common mistake made when a car slips off the edge of a road is to overcorrect by turning the vehicle too sharply in an attempt to get back onto the road. The forward speed of the car and a tire catching the road's edge can cause a rollover. The faster the speed and the more pronounced a drop-off of the road's edge is, the more challenging slipping off the edge is to correct.

The trick is to not panic and to not overreact. Let off the accelerator pedal and gradually turn the front tire back onto the road's surface. Sport utility vehicles, vans, and trucks are usually more susceptible to a rollover because, compared to a regular car, their center of gravity is higher off the ground.

Underwater Entrapment

Many people fear being trapped underwater in a vehicle. While this does make for a great Hollywood suspense script, it is not a common occurrence, compared to other accident causes. Government statistics show the actual number of people that die annually from being trapped underwater in a vehicle is less than 300. This is a very small percentage of total automobile deaths.

Thinking two steps ahead will hopefully prevent this situation from even occurring. Though these types of accidents are rare, they do happen and can instantly ignite decision compression, chaos, and panic within all occupants trapped in the car.

A few things to remember are that unless a window or windshield is broken or open, the car will not instantly fill with water and sink. It will take time for the water to filter into the interior via the air ducts and non-watertight door and window seals. Take immediate note of the outside water level and determine if you are sinking in several feet of water or are resting in shallow water just a few feet deep. Determining if you are sinking determines your course of action. If the car is not sinking and has come to rest above the water line in shallow water, take your time evacuating or wait for extraction.

If, however, the car is sinking, time is obviously of the essence and fast action needs to be taken. It is recommended that the first step is to unlock the doors and then have all occupants remove their seat belts so they can move about freely. Since many cars have door locks that are electrically operated, it important to get them unlocked quickly should the electrical system fail. Outside water pressure will make it difficult or near impossible to push a door open when the inside of the car has air and the outside of the car is surrounded by water pushing against the doors. Opening a window or breaking the glass is usually a good way to exit. Quickly get a window down prior to losing electrical power due to a short.

If you are not able to get a window down, there are still two options remaining even if electrical power is lost. Kicking out or breaking an automobile window is difficult under normal situations due the coatings and strength of the glass material. This usually leaves the options of opening the door or breaking the window glass with a special window-glass tool designed for these situations.

To escape through a door, you have to deal with the outside water pressure pushing the door closed. Pressure will not equalize until most of the trapped air inside of the car is displaced with water. This will happen when the car almost completely fills with water—not a comforting scenario for trapped people. However, it might be your best option. If unable to push a door open, wait until the car is almost completely filled with water. Once the car is mostly filled with water, the pressure differential is reduced to the point that the door can be pushed open. This is risky and a traumatic scenario but there will still be pockets of air from which to breathe. If the car is resting right side up, then the air pockets will be near the inside ceiling of the car. Conversely, if the car is resting upside down, then the air pockets from which to breathe will be near the floorboard of car because the air, which is lighter than water, is trying to float towards the surface.

Consider an old scuba-diving trick. Air bubbles will always float upward to the surface. If it is dark or murky and you are disoriented, blow a few tiny air bubbles out from your mouth while underwater and observe which direction they float. They will always float to and point you toward the surface.

The second option if you are not able to open the window or push the door open is to break the glass. A tool that firefighters and rescue personnel carry is called a window punch. I highly recommend every vehicle has one taped to the inside lid of the console box or to a door pocket. Don't just set it loose somewhere in the vehicle; secure it so it will not move around and get lost during an accident. These spring-loaded punches are inexpensive, easy to use, and are designed specifically for shattering auto glass. Please note that they work best on door windows. Their effectiveness is limited when attempting to punch or shatter the windshield or rear window glass because these windows have different coatings that make shattering the glass more difficult.

Pushing the tip of this spring-loaded tool firmly against a door window will deliver enough pinpoint pressure to shatter the glass. Be aware that by using this tool on a door window that the glass shatters into hundreds of sharp pieces or nuggets. In addition, there is now outside water rushing inward and carrying the shattered glass toward the inside occupants. If possible, place some protection like a jacket or towel over your face prior to shattering the glass. Breaking a window by this method is quick and easy and you do not have to wait for pressure equalization. You can use it at any time. If a window punch is not present, try using an object with a sharp point to apply concentrated pressure to the glass. For example, placing the point of a pen against the glass then using a shoe heel like a hammer to hit the pen may deliver the necessary blow to shatter the glass. It does not take a high-impact accident to bend the car frame enough to jam the doors shut. It is very difficult to open doors bent in a collision. Window punches work great for breaking glass from a collision in addition to being under water.

Blind Spots

I want to re-address blind spots again in a bit more detail. Every vehicle has blind spots and these blind spots slightly change depending on how the driver is positioned. Blind spots are underlying causes of many collisions simply because the driver is prevented from directly seeing another vehicle or person before making a turn or lane change. In fact, 35 percent of all car/truck accidents resulting in fatalities occur in the blind spots of trucks and nearly 70 percent of these crashes are initiated by the driver of a car.[3] Motorcycles can also hide in a car's blind spots because they have a small profile and riders can ride near the edge of a lane.

Accidents which are caused by not seeing a vehicle that is hiding in a blind spot occur in and around intersections and while vehicles are merging onto highways and making lane changes. A common error made by drivers, especially younger drivers, is assuming that side mirrors show everything to the side of the car. This is incorrect.

There are also two major forward blind spots to the front of each side of the car. These are caused by a vision obstruction caused by the support structure for the car's roof. These blind spots are smaller in area, but they sometimes make seeing pedestrians in crosswalks and standing at intersections difficult. These forward blind spots also make it particularly challenging to see vehicles in front during nighttime or in the sun's glare.

In addition to blind spot mirrors, panoramic inside rearview mirrors can be easily added to the existing rearview mirror. These are great for enhancing viewing area in the blind spot behind your vehicle.

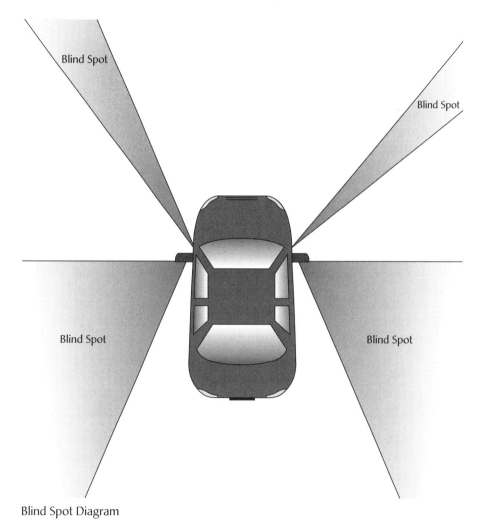

Blind Spot Diagram

Roadside Hazards

Having a flat tire or a car breakdown will usually mean pulling over to the side of a road. Nearly 2,000 people die each year in highway shoulder collisions.[4] When possible, it is best to avoid pulling over to a shoulder that is along a bend in the road, just prior to an intersection, or just prior to an exit lane off of a highway. Being on the side of the road is dangerous enough with 3,000-pound metal cars whizzing by at 50+ miles per hour. However, pulling over on the shoulder of a road that is curving around a bend is particularly dangerous. Drivers following will see the vehicle much later than if it was pulled over on a straight road. This gives other drivers less reaction time to detect and avoid the stopped vehicle.

As we learned, the tendency of a car moving fast around a curve is to move to the outside of the turn. If they are speeding or on wet roads, the tendency will further increase the chances for the car to slide off of the road and onto the same shoulder where you are parked. Think ahead, anticipate, and expect the unexpected.

Similarly, pulling off onto a shoulder just prior to an intersection or an exit ramp is also asking for trouble. A driver planning to turn or exit at the upcoming ramp or intersection has a tendency to naturally drift toward that exit or turning lane prior to actually getting there. Hence, they will have a tendency to migrate in your direction. Even though you are on the shoulder, they will be driving in your direction and might accidentally come onto the shoulder. If the driver of a car exiting a freeway is driving under the influence, driving at night, or following a tall semi-truck trailer, the problem could be compounded further.

You can drive slowly on a flat tire. It is not good for the tire or wheel rim but you can do it and should, in fact, do it to avoid having to park on the shoulder at a curve or just prior to an exit ramp or intersection. If you do happen to become stuck in one of these places, put out flares or reflective warning signs to alert approaching drivers.

Visibility

Visibility, especially forward visibility, is important; the more the better. Be vigilant in improving both visibility looking out from the car and other drivers' visibility of you.

Keep all windows clean. Also keep headlights, taillights, brake lights, and mirrors clean. I clean all outside glass and lights every time

I stop for fuel. Keeping the windows, mirrors, and headlights clean improves my visibility. Keeping the tail and brake lights clean makes me more visible to other drivers. I want my brake lights to shine brightly in the face of the person following me.

Take a few minutes to apply a conditioner such as RainX to your windshield. It makes a dramatic improvement in the beading up of and repelling water from the windshield. In addition, it does a great job of improving visibility, especially during rain.

For those of us living in snow country, when brushing snow off of the car, don't just brush a small porthole in front of the driver's eyes. Brush off the entire car. Improve your visibility by fully removing the snow from each and every window. Brushing the snow off of the entire car also improves other drivers' ability to see you. Your lights will be visible, and if you have a dark-colored car, removing the white snow allows the car to contrast against the white background of the snow.

Remove the fuzzy dice and all objects hanging on the rearview mirror. Resist putting window decals on the glass. Do not place maps, coffee mugs, or any other objects on the front dashboard. These objects can directly block a portion of your forward vision. Improve visibility wherever possible.

Review

- Be alert when driving on unfamiliar roads, especially on hilly roads or roads with curves. The radius of some curves gets smaller as the curve continues, resulting in a progressively tighter turn. The speed a car travels when entering a curve can be too great when leaving the curve, forcing the car to slip off the outside edge of the road surface.
- Overcorrecting a car that has slipped off the road surface is a common mistake and is particularly dangerous for larger vehicles with higher centers of gravity.
- Install blind spot mirrors to assist in managing the blind spot areas regular mirrors have.
- Get and secure a window punch for each vehicle. In addition to underwater escapes, they are great to exit a car with jammed doors from a collision. It takes very little force to bend and jam a car door shut.

Part III: Summary

Parents participating in educating their younger drivers can use the following five-step plan to help establish a foundation of knowledge of what to anticipate and how to react to certain situations. These are very important steps in reducing driver-decision error, especially for younger drivers who lack experience.

Developing a parent/child driving and behavior contract is recommended to reinforce the understanding of the risks young drivers face and also what consequences they face if they elect to practice reckless vehicle operation.

Chapter 17
Five Steps to Reducing Driver Error

It is now time to assemble the overview information from each of the thirteen most common causes of teenage driving deaths and build an action plan for our younger driver. It is impossible to make a foolproof plan that will cover all possible scenarios and guarantee driver safety. The objective is to instill a mindset and to devise a strategy that will reduce the probability of younger driver accidents and deaths.

FAA and NTSB studies have led to the design of specific education dedicated to reducing pilot error. We want to adjust some of these strategies to make them relevant to driving and have you help transfer this knowledge while teaching and driving with your child.

I have organized all the previously discussed material into five steps that parents can follow to assist in the transfer of this knowledge. Taking these steps should help to better improve the odds of keeping young drivers safe by increasing their knowledge of common mistakes and better equipping them to deal with decision making.

Step 1: Understanding Risk

There are three important risk concepts we need to summarize here:

1. Risk is dynamic.
2. Risk is cumulative.
3. Risk is often exponential.

Multiple changing variables continuously alter risk and levels of ability to cope with risk. At any given moment, a young driver's attention, awareness, and external factors change, which result in the same task having different levels of risk at different times. Driving home from school one day may be uneventful but driving home the next day may prove disastrous if the student is drowsy and encounters a drunk driver. Same task—entirely different risk level.

As we discussed in the chapter on risk taking, younger drivers tend to view risk on a singular trip-by-trip basis when in reality, the underlying effect is that repeating a risky behavior or reckless action over and over allows associated risk to accumulate. The more a risky behavior is repeated, the higher the risk grows, and over time, will eventually catch up to the driver, perhaps resulting in a traffic citation or accident.

However, keep in mind that even an alert and safe teen driver is still exposed to the thousands of other drivers who continually repeat risky behavior, which in turn causes their chances of an accident to increase; perhaps the safe young driver finds herself involved in sharing the riskier driver's eventual accident. Risk is always present.

Last, we have already discussed many scenarios that have proven that exponential relationships fuel risk:

- Stopping distances exponentially increase as speed increases. As speed doubles, stopping distance quadruples.
- Crash risk increases exponentially as speed increases.
- The effects of alcohol on the body increase exponentially with consumption.
- The likelihood of being involved in a crash increases exponentially with alcohol/drug consumption.

Therefore, it is important to look at an exponential curve and visualize the rapid increase in risk as multiple events compound. Two risky behaviors are much more likely to cause an unfavorable outcome than if each were to happen individually.

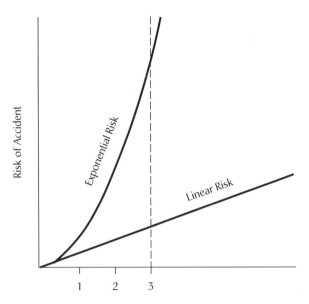

Poor Judgment and Compounding Events

Exponential Risk Diagram

Step 2: Practice the Thirteen Pilot Habits

There are a number of habits that good pilots develop. I have identified thirteen of these many habits that lead to a safer environment and better decision making. These traits can be easily applied to drivers and circumstances encountered while driving.

1. **Anticipate.** Anticipate upcoming events.
2. **Build your outs.** Create a reaction plan to avoid dangerous situations.
3. **Engage in cockpit resource management.** Organize and secure loose items within the vehicle's interior environment.
4. **Err to the conservative.** Choose the least risky alternative.
5. **Be aware of compounding events.** Be aware of events that synergistically compound together to exponentially increase danger.
6. **Expect the unexpected.** Look for the non-obvious event or situation to happen.

7. **Proactively look for trouble.** Try to identify dangerous situations before they fully develop and before they find you.

8. **Develop situational awareness.** Know what is happening around you at all times.

9. **Think two steps ahead.** Know what your next two steps should be. Rehearse what two circumstances are most likely to develop after a given decision is made.

10. **Walk around.** Take a few moments to look around and evaluate your surroundings and vehicle before driving.

11. **See and avoid.** Find potential trouble and make an evasive move to avoid it.

12. **Break the trend.** When a dangerous chain of events starts to develop, break the trend so it does not continue on toward a dangerous outcome.

13. **Avoid get-there-itis.** Avoid being in so much of a rush that you sacrifice safety for the sake of time.

The foundation for improved younger driver safety is to start thinking like a pilot by understanding how these pilot habits can be applied to driving. Beginning to practice these habits in everyday driving situations will raise general awareness and will begin the process of anticipating events. A natural byproduct once a driver starts to anticipate a potential accident or dangerous situation is that he will start formulating outs or ways to avoid risky events.

Step 3: Understand the Five PilotDriver Concepts

I have previously identified five pilotdriver concepts as a result of cross-referencing pilot training, driver training, accident data, and hundreds of statistical reports. I first learned the power and significance of each of these five concepts while flying airplanes and working on a rescue squad. These concepts directly apply to drivers and everyday driving situations. Instruction of younger drivers does not generally address these issues from the point of view of a professionally trained and experienced pilot.

1. **Compounding events.** Events that synergistically compound to exponentially increase danger.

2. **Decision compression.** Being forced to make complex decisions extremely quickly by external forces outside of the driver's control.

3. **Competency silos.** False mental generalizations or attitudes derived from a driver's previous experience lead them to believe they have all the necessary knowledge to make accurate split-second decisions under decision compression and pressure 100% of the time.
4. **Task saturation.** The human brain's inability to process multiple tasks fast enough to keep up with demand.
5. **POP zone defense.** Proactively managing the personal, opportunistic, and participative variables that affect a driver and safe vehicle operation.

These five pilotdriver concepts interact to varying degrees of intensity and complexity for each driving trip made. Given the inexperience level that younger drivers have in both driving and making complex fast decisions, education on these topics helps to build awareness and more importantly, points out a younger driver's vulnerability.

The human brain does not work well in making multiple decisions simultaneously. To compound this deficiency, the younger driver also has inferior driving experience and decision-making practices, which further increase the chance of making a bad decision.

Step 4: Apply PilotDriver Concepts to the Thirteen Young Driver Vulnerabilities

Drivers should practice the thirteen pilot habits for each and every time they are in a vehicle regardless of being the driver or passenger. Secondly, apply the five PilotDriver concepts as needed to make better decisions and manage potentially dangerous situations. Better and safer decisions are the antidote for lowering the 80% error rate in decision making for drivers.

The first four pilotdriver concepts—compounding events, decision compression, competency silos, and task saturation—are concepts to be aware of, anticipate, and then manage. They exist with all drivers and raising awareness of these concepts will help drivers quickly recognize dangerous situations and perhaps take faster corrective action.

The last pilotdriver concept, POP zone defense, is a proactive strategy. It is so powerful and compelling that it will become our blueprint in step 5 as we develop a master plan or checklist to help reduce the probability of younger driver accidents and deaths.

Step 5: Build a Master POP Zone Defense

The three zones of a POP defense:

1. **The personal zone.** The direct control an individual has over his or her body and its ability to act safely.
2. **The opportunistic zone.** A person's immediate environment and his or her ability to influence safety.
3. **The participative zone.** The surrounding environment a person must deal with and which he or she has no personal control over and cannot influence in any way.

If we took the infinite permeations of the thirteen young driver vulnerabilities and dropped them through a make-believe POP zone defense filter, three piles would form. The first pile would consist of vulnerabilities over which the driver has complete control. The second pile would consist of vulnerabilities over which the driver does not have direct control but has some influence over changing. The last pile made from the thirteen young driver vulnerabilities is everything remaining. They are situations for which a driver has no direct control or ability to influence. The driver participates with these variables because they are forced upon him or her.

Now taking these three separate piles of the common ways teenage drivers and passengers get killed, we can make three lists. Each list represents one of the POP zones. The first list is "Personal Zone" and consists of all the vulnerabilities over which a driver or passenger has complete control. The second list is "Opportunistic Zone" and consists of all the vulnerabilities the driver or passenger can either influence or choose to avoid. The last list is "Participative Zone" and consists of all the vulnerabilities that are outside the control of a driver or passenger.

The key point is that there is now a checklist showing the most common ways teenage drivers and passengers get injured or killed, along with an assignment of responsibility and a game plan for increasing the odds of successfully managing each of the three lists or POP zones. This assignment of responsibility creates accountability and with accountability comes the opportunity to demand compliance with rules and practices in an effort to improve the odds of safety. It helps to reinforce the realization that driving is a privilege and certain rules apply. There are, of course, the basic rules that are legally required to drive but these often go against the grain of many teenage attitudes. Beyond these basic rules are the parental rules that are in place to improve a younger driver's chances of safety and overall mortality.

The teenage driver should be held directly responsible for everything stated on the personal zone list; that is those things that they themselves control. Drivers are directly responsible for electing to not drink and drive or take drugs and drive. They are directly responsible for deciding to wear their seat belt. They are directly responsible for not speeding, showing off, driving aggressively, and so forth, and should be held accountable for any and all of these types of actions.

The teenage driver can also be held entirely responsible for all items documented on the opportunistic zone list. Teens can elect not to ride with a drunk driver just like they can elect not to ride with a driver who shows poor judgment. The key here is the opportunity to influence a scenario and to stack the deck further in their favor of remaining safe. This gets somewhat tricky in that a teen may not always know what they are getting into and will most likely make mistakes. Therefore, the parent needs to decide how to evaluate and clearly communicate accurate expectations to the younger driver.

All drivers are forced to deal with the items on the participative zone list. It would be hard and could prove damaging to a relationship for a parent to blame a teen driver for being hit by a drunk driver or being confronted by an enraged driver. It is realistic, however, to expect that young drivers agree to and commit to using some of the thirteen pilot habits in an effort to do their best at driving safely and managing all the events happening alongside of them in their participative zone. Anticipating, thinking two steps ahead, expecting the unexpected, and seeing and avoiding other drivers should be expected behaviors of all drivers as they attempt to avoid confrontations or accidents with irresponsible drivers. This is the best strategy to deal with the participative zone.

This POP zone defense helps identify areas of vulnerability for all drivers and suggests a management strategy for the three POP zones. In addition, it builds a foundation for a teen-parent driving contract.

Table 17.1   Master POP Zone Defense Strategy

Driver's Threat	POP Zone Defense		
	Personal	Opportunistic	Participative
Risk Taking:			
Showing off	✓		
Riding with a driver showing off		✓	
Avoiding a driver showing off			✓
Driving with passengers	✓		
Riding as a passenger of a new driver		✓	
Avoiding a new driver with multiple passengers			✓
Electing to fasten the safety belt	✓		
Driving with multiple teenage passengers	✓		
Riding with a teenage driver and teenage passengers		✓	
Decision Making:			
Deciding to use the IMSAFE checklist	✓		
Driving with an improper attitude	✓		
Riding with a driver exhibiting an improper attitude		✓	
Avoiding a driver with an improper attitude			✓
Driving under task saturation	✓		
Riding with a driver under task saturation		✓	
Avoiding a driver under task saturation			✓
Intersections:			
Scanning and clearing intersections prior to entering	✓		
Timing traffic light duration and changes	✓		
Avoiding running red lights or intersections	✓		
Riding with drivers running red lights or intersections		✓	
Seeing and avoiding other drivers running an intersection			✓
Maintaining lane tracks and make proper changes	✓		
Riding with a driver making improper lane tracks and changes		✓	
Avoiding a driver making improper lane tracks and changes			✓

(continued)

Driver's Threat	Personal	Opportunistic	Participative
Night Vision:			
Using proper day and night vision viewing tactics	✓		
Riding with a driver not using proper day and night vision viewing tactics		✓	
Avoiding a driver not using proper day and night vision viewing tactics			✓
DUI:			
Electing not to drive while under the influence	✓		
Electing not to ride with a driver under the influence		✓	
Avoiding a driver under the influence			✓
Electing not to fall into any of the 5 DUI driver traps	✓		
Electing to not ride with a driver in any of the 5 DUI driver traps		✓	
Avoiding drivers engaging in any of the 5 DUI driver traps			✓
Pedestrians:			
Avoiding playing children	✓		
Avoiding pedestrians	✓		
Speeding:			
Electing not to speed	✓		
Riding with a speeding driver		✓	
Avoiding a speeding driver			✓
Drowsy Driving:			
Electing not to drive while drowsy	✓		
Riding with a drowsy driver		✓	
Avoiding a drowsy driver			✓
Distractions:			
Electing to manage complex distractions	✓		
Riding with a driver that cannot manage complex distractions		✓	
Avoiding a driver that cannot manage complex distractions			✓

(continued)

Table 17.1   Master POP Zone Defense Strategy (continued)

Driver's Threat	Personal	Opportunistic	Participative
Road Rage:			
Electing not to drive aggressively	✓		
Riding with an aggressive driver		✓	
Avoiding an aggressive driver			✓
Electing not to exhibit road rage	✓		
Riding with a driver showing road rage tendencies		✓	
Avoiding a driver or other person with road rage			✓
Adverse Weather:			
Understanding weather effects on driving	✓		
Riding with a driver that does not understand weather effects on driving		✓	
Avoiding a driver that does not understand weather effects on driving			✓
Electing not to drive into flash flood water	✓		
Riding with a driver that does not understand flash flood water		✓	
Safely Approaching Your Vehicle:			
Electing to scan your vehicle and its surrounding area prior to approaching	✓		
Driving while leaving outs from carjackers and assailants	✓		
Riding with a driver that fails to build outs from carjackers and assailants		✓	
Vehicle Control:			
Failure to control the vehicle	✓		

Chapter 18
Teen-Parent Contract

Knowing that younger drivers have limited experience, are maturing, are expanding their boundaries, and are susceptible to making bad decisions, how does a parent go about turning them loose to drive? For starters, there are laws stipulating a minimum training curriculum required to earn a drivers license. This provides a starting point, but many people feel that standard minimum driver training is inadequate in preparing younger drivers to safely operate a vehicle—and a documented 80 to 90 percent driver-error rate for teens confirms it. A detailed study of state driver license requirements by the Insurance Institute for Highway Safety concluded that driver licensing requirements "allow a quick and easy route through the learning phase" and do not place enough emphasis on supervised practice and learning. Although state driver training may educate a teenager on operations and the legal basics of driving, it fails to prepare the younger driver due to her inexperience in decision making and her inability to draw knowledge from previous driving experiences.

I obviously agree with the above assessments, and that is why I have written this book. The training I received in order to drive a car and the training I received to fly were significantly different. Both document that 80 percent of accidents are due to poor decision making.

Many states and driving-related organizations have investigated these statistics and are starting to realize the benefits in what has become known as the graduated driving program. I loosely equate this graduated driving program to the progressive training pilots need in order to obtain their private pilot license. A pilot starts off with basic concepts, then flies solo, then flies on cross-country flights, and then is eligible to carry passengers once an FAA written exam and practical flight test or check ride is passed.

Components of graduated driving programs vary and I suspect we will see a lot of legislation changes as their success rates continue to grow. However, a common denominator is the segregation of a new driver's actual learning phase into three stages: (1) learner's permit,

(2) driver's license with restrictions, and finally (3) driver's license with no restrictions.

> **Stage 1: Learner's permit.** Adult supervision is required at all times. Basic driver education is started. In addition to other restrictions and to be eligible to graduate to Stage 2, a driver must remain free of at-fault crashes and convictions for a period of at least six consecutive months. There is zero alcohol tolerance.
>
> **Stage 2: Intermediate license.** Some basic restrictions are lifted such as unsupervised daylight driving. The new driver continues building knowledge and experience. There remains a zero alcohol tolerance and the driver must remain clear of at-fault crashes.
>
> **Stage 3: Full license.** All restrictions are removed except for applicable laws such as zero tolerance for alcohol for drivers under age 21.

New Zealand implemented a graduated driving program in 1987 and Canada's Ontario program became effective in 1994. In addition, the states of Maryland, California, and Oregon have pioneered programs in graduated licensing for new drivers. All have shown promising results in reducing the crash rate of teenage drivers. An Ontario follow-up study reported a 27 percent decrease in the crash rate for drivers age 16 to 19 years.[1] Graduated driver licensing is a great step forward in attempting to match new driver privileges to driver competence and responsibility.

In addition to following a state's graduated driving requirements, parents are encouraged to draft their own personal graduated driving "laws" for their younger driver. Take into account your state's driving restrictions and expand them to help draft a plan that best matches both the ability and tendencies of your new driver.

This is an exercise that parents should first discuss between themselves and build a framework of desired restrictions with associated timelines and non-compliance penalties. Once an outline is generated, involve the younger driver and get his input and feedback. This process helps to get participation buy-in from the younger driver and is usually better received than handing out a set of rules prior to getting any feedback.

It may be encouraging to note that teenage drivers seem to have fairly high levels of support for graduated driving, with acceptance ranging from 60 to 70 percent. In general, older teens reflecting back on their lack of experience when starting out behind the wheel are shown to be even more supportive that those currently under graduated driving restrictions.[2]

Combining a new driver's lack of driving experience and driving knowledge with the thirteen younger driver vulnerabilities presents a great opportunity to set in place a written document or personal contract between new drivers and their parent(s) that outlines parents' rules and regulations for granting the privilege of driving. Take into account such things as:

- Driving requirements (the need for the new driver to commute to school, work, activities, etc.)
- The new driver's personality and track record of respecting rules and authority
- Any known or perceived weaknesses (poor vision, tendencies to panic, etc.)

Now looking back over the master POP Zone Defense checklist, look for areas or risks you want to specifically restrict or monitor. For example, one very risky scenario for a newly licensed teenage driver is driving at night with multiple teenage passengers. This exponentially compounds the issues of night vision, night perception, peer pressure, distractions, and the propensity for risky behavior. Delaying the permission of this high-risk combination and pushing it into the future helps remove younger drivers from this vulnerability and allows them to build greater knowledge and experience prior to driving at night with other teenagers. Step up or gradually increase privileges. In this case, the teen driver must first complete driving solo, then with a single designated friend during the daytime, then any friend during daytime, and finally driving with multiple friends at night.

A suggested teen-parent contract outline can be created by listing each of the personal and opportunistic items from the master POP Zone Defense checklist and have the teen initial each item promising they will not expose themselves to these high-risk activities:

- I will not drink or take drugs and drive.
- I will not ride with a driver who has been drinking or taking drugs.

- I will always wear a seat belt.
- I will not speed.
- It is okay to call you if I find myself in a difficult situation and wish to remove myself from a threat.

After listing these critical items, design a personal graduated driving program with dates and stipulations for completion along with penalties for non-compliance. Review the Master POP Zone Defense checklist and select the items which you feel are most important. For example, if your driver seems very responsible and you feel comfortable that they will respect your requirement of not drinking, speeding, or operating recklessly, then focus your driving contract on building the skills associated with the participate POP zone. This will help build awareness and focus on avoiding the other dangerous drivers. If however, your driver is a thrill seeker and hangs out with friends you feel might encourage risky behavior, then focus the driving contract around forbidding driving with these friends and not operating in a reckless manner. Visit my Web site at www.pilotdriver.com to download a free teen/parent contract outline that you can modify.

The first milestone I reached in my aviation career was earning my solo flight certificate. I still have this certificate hanging on the wall in my office with my other accomplishments and achievement awards. This is a colorful certificate with a cartoon drawing of a mother pilot bird kicking her baby pilot bird, wearing an old leather flying helmet with goggles, out of the nest.

Like a student pilot being released to fly alone, a teenage driver receives that same kick out of the nest as parents release their children to experience the freedom of driving. Flying and driving are a continuous learning process. I hope that reviewing some of these more alarming crash statistics and combining some of the skills that pilots use has provided a new and different perspective on driving safety. Any incremental level of knowledge that a parent can infuse in a child to reduce the 80% decision error made by drivers and improve the odds of avoiding dangerous situations while on the roads benefits everyone.

Notes

Chapter 1

1. U.S. Department of Transportation, National Highway Traffic Safety Administration, *Traffic Safety Facts 2001: Young Drivers.*
2. U.S. Department of Transportation, National Highway Traffic Safety Administration, *Youth Fatal Crash and Alcohol Facts,* 2000.
3. Insurance Institute for Highway Safety, *Beginning Teenage Drivers.*
4. U.S. Department of Transportation, Federal Aviation Administration, *Advisory Circular: Crew Resource Management Training.*
5. Sheehan, John. "Alarming Findings: Task Force Report Yields Insights Into What Causes Accidents."

Chapter 2

1. U.S. Department of Transportation, National Highway Traffic Safety Administration, *Matching Traffic Safety Strategies to Youth Characteristics: A Literature Review of Cognitive Development.*

Chapter 4

1. Insurance Institute for Highway Safety. *Beginning Teenage Drivers.*
2. U.S. Department of Transportation, National Highway Traffic Safety Administration, *Youth DWI and Underage Enforcement.*
3. U.S. Department of Transportation, National Highway Traffic Safety Administration, *Matching Traffic Safety Strategies to Youth Characteristics: A Literature Review of Cognitive Development.*
4. Ibid.
5. Ibid.
6. Ibid.
7. Ibid.
8. Ibid.
9. Ibid.
10. Ibid.

11. U.S. Department of Transportation, Federal Highway Administration, *Traffic Facts 2001: Overview.*
12. U.S. Department of Transportation, National Highway Traffic Safety Administration, *Matching Traffic Safety Strategies to Youth Characteristics: A Literature Review of Cognitive Development.*
13. U.S. Department of Transportation, National Highway Traffic Safety Administration, *Safety Advice for EMS: A Guide to Injury Prevention.*
14. U.S. Department of Transportation, National Highway Traffic Safety Administration, *Matching Traffic Safety Strategies to Youth Characteristics: A Literature Review of Cognitive Development.*
15. Insurance Institute for Highway Safety, *Teenage Passengers in Motor Vehicle Crashes: A Summary of Current Research.*

Chapter 6

1. North Carolina Department of Motor Vehicles, *Controlling Speed.*
2. U.S. Department of Transportation, National Highway Traffic Safety Administration, *Traffic Safety Facts: Speeding.*
3. Ibid.
4. Ibid.
5. Ibid.

Chapter 7

1. Insurance Institute for Highway Safety, *Fatality Facts: Roadside Hazards.*
2. Operation Lifesaver, Inc., *Presenter Statistics.*
3. W&H Main Yards: *Locomotive, Whistle Signals.*
4. Operation Lifesaver, Inc., *Presenter Statistics.*
5. Conrail, *Crossing the Railroad Safely.*
6. Operation Lifesaver, Inc., *Presenter Statistics.*

Chapter 8

1. Gleim, Irvin, *Pilot Handbook: A Comprehensive Text/Reference for all Pilots*, p. 275.
2. Ibid., p. 277.

Chapter 9

1. U.S. Department of Transportation, National Highway Traffic Safety Administration, *Youth Fatal Crash and Alcohol Facts.*

2. American Academy of Pediatrics, *Drinking and Driving, 2003.*
3. U.S. Department of Transportation, National Highway Traffic Safety Administration, *Strategies For Success: Combating Juvenile DUI.*
4. U.S. Department of Transportation, National Highway Safety Administration, *Youth DWI and Underage Drinking.*
5. U.S. Department of Transportation, National Highway Traffic Safety Administration, *Youth Impaired Driving Manual for Sheriffs.*
6. U.S. Department of Transportation, National Highway Traffic Safety Administration, *Youth Fatal Crash and Alcohol Facts, 2000.*
7. California Department of Alcohol and Drug Programs, *Driving Under the Influence: Frequently Asked Questions, 2002.*
8. U.S. Department of Transportation, National Highway Traffic Safety Administration, *Safety Advice for EMS: A Guide to Injury Prevention.*
9. U.S. Department of Transportation, National Highway Traffic Safety Administration, *Marijuana, Alcohol, and Actual Driving Performance.*
10. U.S. Department of Transportation, National Highway Traffic Safety Administration, *Safety Advice for EMS: A Guide to Injury Prevention.*
11. California Department of Alcohol and Drug Programs, *Driving Under the Influence: Frequently Asked Questions, 2002.*
12. New Hampshire Department of Safety, *DWI Statistics.*
13. U.S. Department of Transportation, National Highway Traffic Safety Administration, *Strategies for Success: Combating Juvenile DUI.*
14. U.S. Department of Transportation, National Highway Traffic Safety Administration, *Impaired Perspectives.*

Chapter 10

1. U.S. Department of Transportation, National Highway Traffic Safety Administration, *Walk Alert: National Pedestrian Safety Program Guide.*
2. U.S. Department of Transportation, National Highway Traffic Safety Administration, *Traffic Safety Facts 2001: Pedestrians.*
3. Ibid.
4. U.S. Department of Transportation, National Highway Traffic Safety Administration, *Walk Alert: National Pedestrian Safety Program Guide.*
5. U.S. Department of Transportation, National Highway Traffic Safety Administration, *Traffic Safety Facts 2001: Pedestrians.*

6. *Automobile Accidents: Some Interesting Facts,* www.thevisualexpert.com.
7. U.S. Department of Transportation, National Highway Traffic Safety Administration, *Traffic Safety Facts 2001: Pedalcyclists.*

Chapter 11
1. U.S. Department of Transportation, National Highway Traffic Safety Administration, *The NHTSA &NCSDR Program to Combat Drowsy Driving.*
2. National Highway Traffic Safety Administration, *Drowsy Driving and Automobile Crashes: Reports and Recommendations.*
3. Ibid.
4. AAA Foundation for Traffic Safety, *Can Drivers Avoid Falling Asleep at the Wheel?*
5. U.S. Department of Transportation, National Highway Traffic Safety Administration, *The NHTSA & NCSDR Program to Combat Drowsy Driving.*
6. U.S. Department of Transportation, National Highway Traffic Safety Administration, *Drowsy Driving and Automobile Crashes: Reports and Recommendations.*
7. AAA Foundation for Traffic Safety, *Wake up!*

Chapter 12
1. Insurance Institute for Highway Safety, *Teenage Passengers in Motor Vehicle Crashes: A Summary of Current Research.*

Chapter 13
1. U.S. Department of Transportation, National Highway Traffic Safety Administration, *Strategies for Aggressive Driver Enforcement.*
2. Ibid.
3. U.S. Department of Transportation, National Highway Traffic Safety Administration, *A Driver's Guide to Coping With Congestion.*
4. U.S. Department of Transportation, National Highway Traffic Safety Administration, *Aggressive Drivers Are Often Competitive.*
5. Lerche Davis, Jeanie, "Getting a Grip on Roadway Anger."
6. U.S. Department of Transportation, National Highway Traffic Safety Administration, *Aggressive Drivers Are Often Competitive.*
7. AAA Foundation for Traffic Safety, *Preventing Road Rage: How to Avoid Aggressive Driving.*
8. Ibid.

Chapter 14

1. US Department of Commerce: National Oceanic and Atmospheric Administration, *Flash Floods and Floods . . . the Awesome Power.*
2. Ibid.
3. www.flood2000.com. 2003.
4. Rigg, Nancy, *Swift Water and Flash Flood Safety Tips.*
5. *All Weather Driving Tips,* www.weather.com.
6. www.flood2000.com. 2003.
7. Ibid.
8. *Get into the Habit of Checking Your Vehicle's Tires: 70% of U.S. Drivers Don't Know How to Tell if Tires are Bald,* www.businesswire.com.

Chapter 15

1. McGoey, Chris E., *Carjacking.*
2. Klaus, Patsey, U.S. Department of Justice, Bureau of Justice Statistics, *Carjackings in the United States, 1992-96.*

Chapter 16

1. Insurance Institute for Highway Safety, *Fatality Facts: Roadside Hazards.*
2. Ibid.
3. Ohio Department of Public Safety, *It's About Safety.*
4. U.S. Department of Transportation, National Highway Traffic Safety Administration, *Share the Road Safely.*

Chapter 18

1. U.S. Department of Transportation, National Highway Traffic Safety Administration, *Saving Teenage Lives: A Case for Graduated Driver Licensing.*
2. Ibid.

Bibliography

AAA Foundation for Traffic Safety. *Can Drivers Avoid Falling Asleep at the Wheel?* Washington, D.C.: AAA Foundation for Traffic Safety, 1993.

————. *Preventing Road Rage: How to Avoid Aggressive Driving.* Washington, D.C.: AAA Foundation for Traffic Safety, 2000.

————. *Wake Up!* Washington, D.C.: AAA Foundation for Traffic Safety, 2000.

All Weather Driving Tips. Accessed via Web at www.weather.com, address verified May 13, 2003.

American Academy of Pediatrics. *Drinking and Driving, 2003.* Accessed via Web at www.aap.org, address verified September 26, 2003.

The Angels on Track Foundation. *Railroad Safety.* Accessed via Web at www.angelsontrack.org, address verified January 1, 2004.

Automobile Accidents: Some Interesting Facts. Accessed via Web at www.thevisualexpert.com, address verified May 17, 2003.

California Department of Alcohol and Drug Programs, *Driving Under the Influence: Frequently Asked Questions.* Accessed via Web at www.adp.ca.gov, address verified October 2002.

California Department of Alcohol and Drug Programs. *Driving Under-the-Influence: Statistics.* Accessed via Web at www.adp.ca.gov, address verified October 2002.

Coleman, Christopher D. *W&H Main Yards: Locomotive, Whistle Signals.* Accessed via Web at www.spikesys.com, address verified January 9, 2004.

Conrail. *Crossing the Railroad Safely.* Accessed via Web at www.conrail.com, address verified January 2, 2004.

Get into the Habit of Checking Your Vehicle's Tires: 70% of U.S. Drivers Don't Know How to Tell if Tires Are Bald. Accessed via Web at www.businesswire.com, address verified May 14, 2003.

Gleim, Irvin. *Pilot Handbook: A Comprehensive Text/Reference for All Pilots.* 6th ed. Gleim Publications, Inc. 1999.

Insurance Institute for Highway Safety. *Beginning Teenage Drivers.* Accessed
    via Web at www.hwysafety.org, address verified January 2, 2004.
————. *Fatality Facts: Roadside Hazards.* Accessed via Web at
    www.hwysafety.org, address verified September 6, 2003.
————. *Red Light Running.* Accessed via Web at www.hwysafety.org,
    address verified June 2003.
————. *Teenage Passengers in Motor Vehicle Crashes: A Summary of Cur-
    rent Research.* Accessed via Web at www.hwysafety.org, address
    verified January 2, 2004.
Jeppesen Sanderson, Inc. *Aviation Fundamentals.* Englewood, CO:
    Jeppesen Sanderson Training Products. 1985.
Klaus, Patsey. U.S. Department of Justice, Bureau of Justice Statistics.
    Carjackings in the United States, 1992–96. March 1999.
Lerche Davis, Jeanie. "Getting a Grip on Roadway Anger," *WebMD.*
    Accessed via Web at http://my.webmd.com/content/
    article/35/1728_56860, address verified April 21, 2003.
McGoey, Chris E. *Carjacking.* Accessed via Web at
    www.crimedoctor.com, address verified May 13, 2003.
New Hampshire Department of Safety. *DWI Statistics.* Accessed via
    Web at www.nh-dwi.com, address verified August 2, 2003.
North Carolina Department of Motor Vehicles. *Controlling Speed.*
    Accessed via Web at www.dmv.dot.state.nc.us, address verified
    May 17, 2003.
Ohio Department of Public Safety. *It's About Safety.* November 2001.
Operation Lifesaver Inc. *Presenter Statistics.* Accessed via Web at
    http://server.oli.org, address verified January 8, 2004.
Rigg, Nancy. *Swift Water and Flash Flood Safety Tips.* Accessed via Web
    at www.flood2001.com, address verified May 13, 2003.
Sheehan, John. "Alarming Findings: Task Force Report Yields Insights
    into What Causes Accidents," *AOPA Pilot* (May 2003): 105–110.
U.S. Department of Commerce, National Oceanic and Atmospheric
    Administration. *A Preparedness Guide.* 1992.
U.S. Department of Justice, Office of Justice Programs. *Carjackings in
    the United States, 1992–96.* March 1999.
U.S. Department of Transportation, Federal Aviation Administration.
    Advisory Circular: Crew Resource Management Training. Washing-
    ton, D.C.: U.S. Department of Transportation. February 8, 2001.
U.S. Department of Transportation. Federal Highway Administration.
    Traffic Facts 2001: Overview. Washington, D.C.: U.S. Department
    of Transportation. 2001.

————. *National Agenda for Intersection Safety—Preliminary Draft.* Washington, D.C.: U.S. Department of Transportation.

U.S. Department of Transportation, National Highway Traffic Safety Administration, *Aggressive Drivers Are Often Competitive.* U.S. Department of Transportation. April 1998.

————. *A Driver's Guide to Coping with Congestion.* July 1998.

————. *Driving After Drug or Alcohol Use: Findings from the 1966 National Household Survey on Drug Abuse.* December 1998.

————. *Drowsy Driving and Automobile Crashes: Reports and Recommendations.* 1998.

————. *Impaired Perspectives.* May 1998.

————. *Marijuana, Alcohol, and Actual Driving Performance.* 1999.

————. *Matching Traffic Safety Strategies to Youth Characteristics: A Literature Review of Cognitive Development.* June 1999.

————. *The NHTSA and NCSDR Program to Combat Drowsy Driving.* March 1999.

————. *Safety Advice for EMS—A Guide to Injury Prevention.* Washington, D.C.: 1996.

————. *Saving Teenage Lives: A Case for Graduated Driver Licensing.* November 1998.

————. *Share the Road Safely.* 1998.

————. *Strategies for Aggressive Driver Enforcement.* 1998.

————. *Strategies for Success: Combating Juvenile DUI.* August 1999.

————. *Traffic Safety Facts 2001: Alcohol.* 2001.

————. *Traffic Safety Facts 2001: Pedalcyclists.* 2001.

————. *Traffic Safety Facts 2001: Pedestrians.* 2001.

————. *Traffic Safety Facts 2001: Speeding.*

————. *Traffic Safety Facts 2001: Young Drivers.* Washington, D.C.: 2001.

————. *The Visual Detection of DWI Motorists.*

————. *Walk Alert: National Pedestrian Safety Program Guide.*

————. *Youth DWI and Underage Enforcement.* 1998.

————. *Youth Impaired Driving Manual for Sheriffs.* 2001.

————. *Youth Fatal Crash and Alcohol Facts 2000.* Washington, D.C.: January 2002.

Glossary

ADM (Aeronautical Decision Making)—A structured thinking process used by pilots to evaluate a given set of circumstances and consistently deduce the most appropriate course of action.

BAC (blood alcohol concentration)—The standard measure of blood alcohol concentration in a person's body.

Competency silo—An individual's false belief and generalization that they are capable of appropriately reacting to any given situation based on limited previous experience.

Compounding events—Multiple variables that synergistically interact to cause a given situation to quickly grow in risk and complexity.

Crunch time—A period requiring extreme concentration as a pilot completes multiple tasks and makes multiple decisions in a very short amount of time.

Decision compression—When variables outside of a driver's control force a complex evaluation of possible appropriate actions that are further complicated by the driver's vehicle being in motion.

Dew point—The temperature at which air cools to enable the presence of visible moisture.

Enroute—The established cruising phase of a flight between takeoff and landing.

G-Forces—The forces of acceleration that pull on an object due to a change in the plane of motion. An airplane in a banking turn or a person in a car traveling around a turn in the road will experience an increase in G-force.

Glide slope—Vertical guidance information transmitted by an airport's instrument landing system that is received by aircraft instrumentation and allows a pilot to make a structured descent to the runway.

IFR (instrument flight rules)—A set of regulations that permit a properly trained pilot to control an aircraft by reference solely to cockpit instrumentation.

Instrument rated—An endorsement to a pilot's license permitting the control of an aircraft's flight by reference solely to cockpit instrumentation.

Minimum descent altitude—The lowest altitude a pilot is permitted to fly for a given runway in an attempt to visually acquire that runway in poor visibility.

PIREP (*pilot reports*)—Information filed by pilots and made available to other pilots seeking information about a particular location or set of conditions.

POP zone defense—A strategy for risk management combining the associated personal, *o*pportunistic and participative variables.

Skin effect—The tendency for alternating current to flow mostly near the outer surface of an electrical conductor, such as metal wire or a metal automobile body.

Task saturation—A point at which the human brain becomes incapable of keeping pace with the demand for making numerous and immediate decisions.

VFR (visual flight rules)—A set of regulations that permit a properly trained pilot to control an aircraft by visual reference to the ground and horizon.

Wind shear—An abrupt and significant change in wind direction and/or speed potentially preventing an airplane's ability to maintain controlled flight.

Index

Boldface page numbers refer to figures and tables

Order Form

Name: _____

Mailing Address: _____

_____

City & State: _____

Zip Code: _____

Telephone: _____

Fax: _____

E-mail: _____

Please send _____ copy (copies) of ***Saving Our Teen Drivers: Using Aviation Safety Skills on the Roadways*** @ $19.95 per copy, please add $5.00 (shipping and handling) and 7.25% (sales tax).

Please bill my credit card.

Credit card: Visa ❑ MC ❑ Amex ❑

Card No: _____

Exp date: _____

Signature of cardholder: _____

Code: _____

Please mail your order form to:

BookMasters, Inc.
30 Amberwood Parkway
Ashland, OH 44805
800-247-6553

You may fax your order to: 419-281-6883

E-mail your order to: order@bookmasters.com

Order through our web site: http://www.atlasbooks.com

Visit www.pilotdriver.com for more driving safety information